THE POWER AND THE KINGDOM

The Power
and
The Kingdom

A Personal Look at Power, Politics
and the Book of Revelation

MICHAEL WILLIAMS

MONARCH
Eastbourne

Front cover photos:
Background: Network Photographers
Top colour: Susan Criggs Agency
Bottom colour: Zefa Picture Library

British Library cataloguing in publication data

Williams, Michael, *1942–*
   The power and the kingdom.
   I. Title
   228'.06

ISBN 1–85424–035–8

Printed in Great Britain for
MONARCH PUBLICATIONS LTD.
1, St Anne's Road, Eastbourne, E Sussex BN21 3UN by
Richard Clay Ltd, Bungay, Suffolk.
Typeset by J&L Composition, Filey, N. Yorks.

To Miranda

Acknowledgements

This book draws on insights and experiences stretching back to 1970 when I went to share in the work of the Toxteth Team Ministry as a curate. My first thanks must therefore go to all those colleagues who worked with me in that team and to the members of the several congregations that we tried to serve.

On leaving Liverpool to teach in Durham, I joined a new staff team and I thank them for their patience with me as I attempted to incorporate insights from urban ministry into the theological curriculum. In particular, I must thank the leader of the team, Miss Ruth Etchells, for her personal support and encouragement. She gave me space to explore the urban and political issues considered in this book and it was also under her Principalship that the College set up an Urban Studies Centre in Gateshead.

The bulk of the work on the text for this book was written in the autumn of 1987 when I was given a sabbatical term. I thank the Council of St John's College for this opportunity.

Finally, my thanks go to Mrs Gwen Bayley for so carefully typing the manuscript.

MICHAEL WILLIAMS

CONTENTS

Foreword: a Book of Hope

The debate about the relationship between the church and the political arena, though lengthy, shows no sign of abating. One of its difficulties is its over-simplicifaction: almost as though the world we inhabit has absolutely clear demarcation limits, and a great gulf fixed between humankind as political beings and humankind as spiritual beings.

But the supreme wonder of the Incarnation of Our Lord Jesus Christ is that he took into himself the whole of humankind in its nature, as well as its extent. So he blessed and redeemed and made new the possibilities of humanity in its social and political manifestations, pointing to their rootedness in the nature of man the fallen and redeemed image of God himself.

So vast a redeeming refuses to locate itself in the narrow vision and ideology of any one political party or social programme or even in any one civilisation. All time and beyond time is its context: and social and political programmes have to be judged against that background.

Hence the Book of Revelation, that last and enigmatic book of the Bible, challenges as one and the same text to think of the redemption of Jesus Christ in its eternal aspect, beyond time, and its particular timely aspect, as it applies not simply to our world today, but to this particular moment in this particular social and political context.

No one could be better equipped than Michael Williams to hold these two paradoxical elements together. His experience as vicar of a parish in the Toxteth area of Liverpool, and initiator of an exciting new Urban Studies Unit for the training of ordinands in Gateshead, has been sieved and fine tuned in his experience for ten years as Director of Pastoral Studies in Cranmer Hall, St John's College, Durham. The effect of that has been to confirm his refusal to take on the jargon or the uncritical assumptions of any social programme or political party, but rather to hold all such promises and condemnations under the strong searchlight of the word of God: in this particular case, focused through his study of the Book of Revelation.

For though Michael Williams minds deeply about the disadvantaged, he also cares passionately about clear thinking. So these two are the dynamics of this book, which is shaped by wide and eclectic reading, a glorious sense of humour, a most vivid turn of phrase (see 'lion' and 'lamb' power, for example) and a deeply pastoral Christian faith.

Hence this book is both courageous and extraordinarily readable. I found it compulsive – not least because it is gloriously free of theological jargon as well as the political and the sociological. In it he helps us, with gentle but relentless integrity, to face as Christians our political, social and moral dilemmas as spiritual beings, both corporately and individually. The conclusions he inexorably draws us to are not easy ones: this is a brave book. But at the same time it is an encouraging and inspiring one, for it is an exercise in constantly putting our thinking under God's judgement and grace alike, and there finding our resources. He writes, 'Because justice is part of God's holy nature, judgement cannot be evaded. This does not mean, however, that God puts off his mercy and cloaks himself with revenge. Rather, God judges from his mercy and on his mercy alone.'

Hence, Michael Williams' message is ultimately one of utmost hope.

The book grew from three meditations on the Book of Revelation, given in the Chapel of St John's College. Readers will discover, as his ordinand students have in that College, (and will in the Northern Ordination Course where he is now Principal) that the clarity, directness, humour and profundity of what Michael has to say about living as Christians in our times, is rooted in his life of worship and his wrestling with the biblical text. I am delighted that a wider world is to share the challenge; and I am deeply privileged to commend it.

RUTH ETCHELLS

CHAPTER ONE

MY WAY IN

IN FEBRUARY 1986 Miss Ruth Etchells, the Principal of St John's College, Durham, asked me to give three Bible expositions in the college chapel. At that time I was preoccupied by the *Faith in the City* report published by the Church of England, and so I decided to preach on a biblical text which would address some of the social and political issues raised by it. During my inner-city ministry in Toxteth (1970–78), the Book of Revelation had been a great source of strength to me, precisely because it so penetratingly illuminates the themes of power and dominion, so I naturally found myself turning to it for the expositions. After I had given these sermons, Ruth suggested that a wider audience might appreciate them. So I expanded and developed them and the result is this book.

So very often Bible commentaries do a good job in explaining the text, but they don't seem to reach right into our modern situation. The questions which we face in our ordinary lives at work, in the family, and as citizens in the political and social process don't seem to get answered when we consult them. There often seems to be a huge gap between the world of the early Christians and our technological age. Even when commentaries apply the words of Scripture to our present questions, they seem much better at addressing issues of private faith than helping us face the political realities of the day. And when political questions are addressed, they are usually tackled in very simplistic ways such as suggesting that the Beast of Revelation is really Stalin or Hitler or some other historical figure. In trying to allow the text of Revelation to speak to the reality of our present social and political situation, I had to develop my own method which would avoid these pitfalls.

What I have chosen to do is to take three fundamental themes from Revelation: the Lamb, the Beasts and the Millennium, and begin to draw out their significance for our political life here and now. I chose this particular method for several reasons, the most important being my conviction that underlying the political views espoused by political parties, governments and movements lie deeply-held ideals that are more than simply economic theories. Our political situation is extremely complex, but the policies that particular parties advocate seem to me to have two levels to them. The first level is economic theory, but the deeper level is the fundamental values and judgements from which the economic theory springs. This two-level analysis helps to explain why different economists and politicians can look at the same situation or the same set of statistics and see two quite different solutions. Our deeply-held views influence us more than we perhaps admit. In any case, the science of economics is not an exact science and so we rely more on fundamental value judgements than on the conflicting economic predictions.

My method in this book has therefore been to try to unearth some of the more fundamental political themes that we see abroad today and compare them with my three chosen themes from the Book of Revelation. This explains why the resulting book is neither a detailed exposition of the text of Revelation nor a statistical analysis of our present political world. I have used some statistics and I have expounded some of the text in detail, but my overall attempt has been to compare the major themes of Revelation with the major themes of present politics.

That such an approach is justified I take to be vindicated by the Prime Minister's speech to the General Assembly of the Church of Scotland (21st May, 1988). Her address was a sincere attempt to state her own fundamental values as a Christian. She made it clear that it was these very values that she tried to make the basis of her particular political philosophy. She chose to concentrate on freedom of choice, individual responsibility, the necessity for hard work, and the creation of wealth. Some critics of her speech accused her of cynicism — just using certain biblical texts and passages to hang Conservative party policy on. But such critics miss the mark. What we have in that speech is a genuine attempt by one politician to lay bare her fundamental value system. We see from the speech that what really motivates her is not just particular economic theories, but deeply held social values.

In what follows I have tried to expose not just the fundamental values of particular politicians, but also to look at our culture as a whole. This is why I have used secular critics from the arts such as Tolstoy, Camus and Golding. Economists and political philosphers don't, in my opinion, have the same power to penetrate to the deep values of life as do artists and visionaries. To the careful student of Tolstoy and the other writers, the use that I make of their work may seem irresponsible, but I would justify myself by saying that I have used their stories to illustrate my themes rather than to offer a correct exegesis of their text. I have made no attempt to pretend to be a literary critic. Instead I have taken the stories of Caligula and the Dean etc to throw light on the themes I wanted to develop. Once an artist writes a story it becomes a public possession. What I have said in the pages that follow has less to do with the author's intentions and more to do with my own wrestling with the characters that they have created. Mine has been a living dialogue with these stories, not a strictly academic one. The same is true of my references to DH Lawrence. My primary concern has been to take seriously his critique of the

Book of Revelation in his own commentary, *Apocalypse*. This book and *Etruscan Places* reflect a particular facet of his character which raises questions about the Book of Revelation. An expert in Lawrence's work would probably find my picture of him one-sided, but this is the side of him that I wanted to engage with because it illuminates the deep political values that I want to expose.

As a way of bringing together the three biblical themes and the modern political themes, I have used my own experience. This makes the book a very personal reflection on the nature of power and Christian social action. It is held together by my own personal involvement in the struggles of one inner-city community and my present grappling with the issues of the North/South divide. It in no way claims to be a blueprint for Christian lifestyle and social action. The disadvantage of using my own story to integrate the themes is that it risks coming across to others as a biased selection of insights, but I would defend my approach to the hilt because politics and social action are, in the end, about our own commitment to involvement rather than armchair theorising.

Although I have used a variety of commentaries on the Book of Revelation, I am most indebted to Caird's. I discovered this commentary during my time in inner-city Liverpool and his interpretation of the text was a great inspiration to me. Revelation spoke to me and the members of my church through this commentary precisely because Caird exposes the themes of power, freedom and responsibility. His analysis of providence brought hope to an often hopeless situation.

Inner-city life and ministry is about power. It is about who has power and who does not have power. It is about how Christians ought to react to being at the mercy of those politicians who hold the power. As I pondered on the message of Revelation, I came to realise that despite the evidence all around me, God was still King.

Political power, especially in modern democratic countries, is closely connected with cultural values. Democratic governments depend on popular support, so they only retain power as long as their overall policies reflect the prevailing values among the electorate. This is why I have spent a considerable amount of time in this study of Revelation trying to assess current social values. There can be no doubt that the 1980s have seen a return to entrepreneurial values and pre-Keynesian economics. I have tended to refer here to such values as Western because they seem to have such prominence in the United States and Great Britain, but Reaganomics and Thatcherism are only two examples of a wider movement. The economies and cultures of such widely differing countries as Australia, Japan, India and Korea are also affected. The biblical reservations that I express in this book about Western values do, therefore, have much wider significance.

The Lamb

Judgement Begins at Home
Revelation chapters 1–3

CHAPTER TWO

WIND IN THE WILLOWS?

'WHAT ARE YOU TALKING ABOUT? Do you mean to say you haven't *heard*?'

'Heard what?' said Toad, turning rather pale. 'Go on, Ratty! Quick! Don't spare me! What haven't I heard?'

'Do you mean to tell me,' shouted the Rat, thumping his little fist upon the table, 'that you've heard nothing about the Stoats and Weasels?'

'What, the Wild Wooders?' cried Toad, trembling in every limb 'No, not a word! What have they been doing?'

' — And how they've been and taken Toad Hall?' continued the Rat.

What a sorry homecoming Mr Toad has! Having just escaped from prison, where he has been 'unjustly' interned for 'borrowing' a motor car, he returns to his country mansion, the finest residence for miles around, only to find that it has been taken over by the stoats and weasels. These wild animals of the wood cannot be trusted. They are always waiting for an opportunity to break out, to take over, to grab what is not theirs and deprive the rightful owners of their privilege. Their power lies in their numbers and their sharp teeth. They are consumed by envy for the wealth of others and are constantly driven to seek it for themselves. They have swarmed out of the Wild Wood and taken over Toad Hall, desecrating everything by their savage and scornful behaviour and rejoicing in the downfall of Mr Toad.

Kenneth Grahame's *The Wind in the Willows* is more than a children's story. It is also a social and political statement. In the book the sly fox, the envious stoat and the grasping weasel represent the lower levels of society. They desire the wealth and status of those above them in the social order and lie in wait to grab it for themselves. For the moment they have succeeded — they possess Mr Toad's ancestral home. But the story does not end there. In a daring Ulyssean attack, Mr Toad and his friends reclaim their rightful place in society and Toad Hall is repossessed.

Such a jaundiced view of the English working class of the late nineteenth and early twentieth centuries serves to remind us that we are all conditioned by our background and culture in the way in which we look at the world. All of us have our prejudices and they colour the facts as we perceive them. The spectacles that we wear distort the truth and such distortions can have very grave social consequences if they are shared by a large enough group. Regarding the lower classes as the enemy of civilisation only breeds distrust and exacerbates class warfare. It prevents any clear social analysis and takes refuge in dogmatism. Its mirror image, namely that 'the bosses are always against the workers', is equally dangerous, because it prevents real dialogue and exchange.

I begin this book on political themes in the book of Revelation with a warning about naïve social prejudice in order to challenge us to lay aside our own prejudices, whatever they may be, so that we might arrive at a clearer understanding of the issues involved. None of us can divorce ourselves from our particular political and social roots, nor would it be right for us to do so, but we ought to be able to lay aside the more negative and destructive aspects of our heritage. Only as we struggle to do this will God's word break forth among us.

To recognise that we view both Scripture and life through spectacles coloured by our own social prejudices is of crucial importance if we are to come to terms with the social teaching of the Bible. It is only as we begin to take account of our presuppositions that we realise just how much they colour what we read in the text. We must therefore be willing to explore our own system of values and be prepared for Scripture to call them into question.

Grahame's particular social prejudice of an envious working class is of special relevance to the study of Revelation because it helps us to understand why so many people have rejected the book as being far too brutal to be Christian. One of the best statements of this position is contained in DH Lawrence's commentary, *Apocalypse*. Lawrence sees the martyrs of Revelation as being nothing more than lower-class people who want to turn the tables on their oppressors. He thought that the book had been written for the early Christians, who were powerless and persecuted, to encourage them to think that one day they would be top dogs. The message in a nutshell is: 'Don't worry about being persecuted now brothers, because one day you will be on top and God will give you power to grind your persecutors into the dust.'

The kind of Christianity portrayed in Revelation is, according to Lawrence, the kind of Christianity that he heard preached in the Primitive Methodist chapels of his boyhood. It is a Christianity of envy and greed for power. A powerful image colours his picture both of Revelation and of the working classes of his day. It is a Christian Methodist miner who stands with his foot on the neck of the mine owner who oppressed him in earthly life.

It is this brutal image which dominated and coloured Lawrence's thinking about Christianity and about Revelation in particular. He was specially angry about the book, angry

enough to make *Apocalypse* his dying manifesto, because he
thought that John had used the very ancient images of blood,
horns, virgins, beasts and dragons, and twisted them to portray
a materialistic and envious faith. To Lawrence these images
were precious because they went back to the dawn of time and
spoke to him of a world where human beings were close to
nature, in touch with their sexuality, and free from the
mercenary and industrial ugliness of his own day. He saw it
almost as sacrilege for John to have taken these symbols
and turned them into a propagandist tract whose purpose was
to portray a mean and envious Christianity as ultimately
victorious.

If the martyrs of Revelation are simply the downtrodden
masses who are just waiting to avenge themselves against their
oppressors, and if the God of Revelation is the kind of Being
who glories in punishment and torture in order to establish his
rule, then Lawrence and reformers like Luther were right to
reject the book. It can have no place in the Christian canon if
these are its themes. But my argument is that the theology of
Revelation is not like that at all. It portrays a God who suffers
with his people, and martyrs who willingly shed their own
blood and not the blood of others. If I am right, then a serious
question remains as to why someone like Lawrence could so
systematically misunderstand the central message of the book.
The answer must surely be that his own distorted image of
Christianity, together with his own social prejudices and
presuppositions, led him to read the book in a very distorted
light. We must, therefore, take every care to avoid the same
pitfall by asking the Holy Spirit to lead us to the truth.

CHAPTER THREE

LAMB POWER

THE CONCEPT OF ENVY prevented Lawrence from unlocking the treasure to be found in the Book of Revelation. Where shall we begin to look for the key? The answer must be in the example of our Lord himself.

Before his public ministry began, Jesus had to face the issue of power and how he would use it. In the wilderness he underwent an intense spiritual battle. He knew he was called to be the Saviour of the world, but the question he wrestled with here was how that ministry would be exercised. The key question is the question of power. In coming face to face with that question Jesus highlights some vital precepts about the way in which power should be handled in any context. The way in which a parent uses power in the family; the way in which a teacher uses power in the classroom; the way in which the clergy use power in the church; and the ways in which politicians and civil servants use power — all these uses of power are challenged by the way in which Jesus faced his temptations. His struggle in the wilderness was not just confined to the spiritual and personal realm. It touched every dimension we are all involved in whenever we exercise power or even think about it.

Jesus' first temptation was to be a bread-giving Messiah.

When, daily, we see pictures of starving children in our newspapers and on television, it is very natural to draw the conclusion that the world certainly does need a bread-giving Messiah. I experienced real depression in the year of the great Ethiopian famine when we saw nightly on our television screens the appalling suffering of those starving people. Although one could give sacrificially to aid programmes, somehow that didn't seem enough. The cause of this famine, as of other famines, was more complex, being deeply political. Against such odds I felt powerless and this powerlessness turned into depression because I began to get angry with God. I felt that it was too simple to blame human beings — surely God must take some of the blame? It wasn't long before my picture of the loving, caring God of Christianity began to be replaced by that of a cruel tyrant coldly watching his children suffer. My prayers mainly consisted of an angry cry to God for a bread-giving Messiah.

Looking back I'm glad that, in his mercy, God allowed me to pray those angry prayers because they kept me in touch with the God who would lead me through the same spiritual struggle that our Lord went through in the wilderness. Jesus knew all about poverty and starvation, yet he rejected the call to be a bread-giving Messiah. And because he is like his Father, merciful and compassionate, this must have taken him all his spiritual strength. The account of Jesus' temptations in the Gospels is just a few verses but we must not forget the intensity and duration of the struggle.

Jesus refused to be a bread-giving Messiah because he refused to use power in that way. To buy people's affection and loyalty, and to buy the obedience of the human race would have been a misuse of divine power. True satisfaction, which is not just a matter of bread for our bellies but includes all our emotional, mental and spiritual needs as well, can never come, apart from receiving the whole word of God and living by it. Sometimes our Lord's resistance to this first temptation is interpreted as implying that physical needs are only secondary to spiritual ones. But this is a misunderstanding that borders on blasphemy. God does care for the created world and *all* his children's needs, but he knows that there can never be true salvation and fulfilment until people learn to worship him freely and without being bought. The future of the world, indeed the whole of creation, depends upon the Messiah not using power in this way. None of us can imagine the cost of this decision on the part of a compassionate and caring God. It was a cost that was only truly revealed in the cross.

If our Lord refused to use power in this way, then so must we. We must never use power to buy people's loyalty or meet people's immediate needs while ignoring longer-term needs. In the family this means allowing our children to face up to life's difficulties for themselves instead of trying to solve all their problems for them. In the social and political spheres it means rejecting any use of power that tends to create dependency.

The intention of the English public housing dream, which spawned large council housing estates in and around our towns and cities, was laudable enough in itself. The aim was to ensure that all citizens, no matter what their means, should have a decent place to live. But because those who were rehoused were often given only very limited choice, the end result has been the creation of dependency in many communities. The more recent policy of the sale of such council houses to sitting tenants is only a very crude response to such dependency because it does not touch the most problematic communities. The third alternative of housing associations stands a better chance, but it is only very recently that such schemes are beginning to be funded at levels that have any chance of touching the real problems.

The second temptation that Jesus faced was to become a signs and wonders Messiah. Signs and wonders are an integral part of the biblical witness, even though some liberal scholars have tried to show that such phenomena are only the superstitious wrappings of the gospel. Their attempts fail because as soon as they begin to remove the miraculous elements from the four Gospels the narratives themselves cease to be intelligible. The picture of Jesus left by such a process may be more acceptable to modern liberal minds, but it would certainly not fit into a first-century context. Other Christians have tried to argue that such signs were only meant for the first generation of believers, but that is to squeeze God into our human way of thinking.

However, despite the fact that signs and wonders are such a fundamental part of the gospel, Jesus still refused to be a signs and wonders Messiah because he will not use his power or privilege as Son of God to blackmail people into believing. To try to blackmail people into belief is to dehumanise them because it seeks to override the individual's right to withhold their trust. Our Lord's many miracles did not automatically produce faith in those who witnessed them. The record shows that there were those who saw them as displays of demonic power, and, as for the rest, it is safe to assume that very few who were healed actually saw the meaning of the sign. That wing of the charismatic movement which stresses signs and wonders as evidence of God at work must take Jesus' second temptation seriously.

Signs and wonders themselves do not produce faith, and to try to make them do so is to misunderstand and misuse power. The proper role that such miracles do have in the kingdom of God is to point us to the true nature of the King. They are like signposts, drawing our attention to the nature of God as Liberator. When we find ourselves released from our bondages and when we see others freed from evil and sickness, so our eyes are directed towards the One who delivers us but, like signposts, they do not force us to follow a particular direction. It is clear from the Gospels that Jesus' own miracles were understood only by some, others even tried to turn them against him.

In his second test Jesus was faced not only with the temptation to blackmail people into belief but also to blackmail

God into action. To jump off the pinnacle of the Temple would have been to blackmail God into doing something dramatic before he reached the bottom; it would have been the classic attempt to twist God's arm.

As I read *Fear No Evil* (Hodder and Stoughton: London, 1984), the moving story of David Watson's personal struggle with cancer, I couldn't help thinking that some of those who were convinced that he would get well were very close to falling prey to this temptation. In David Watson's death we are reminded that although we have absolute confidence in God's power to heal, we must always leave the outcome in his almighty hands. It is only in this way that grace can truly remain grace. Such a way of thinking is the opposite of fatalism because it is based on an absolute trust in a loving Father who cares for his children. In this sense, perhaps the ministry that David Watson had in his death will be even greater than that which he had in his life because it shows that no one can blackmail God into action. We must put God's kingdom first, even before signs and wonders.

The danger of using power to blackmail is not only present in the area of supernatural miracles, but also in political life and in our personal relationships. When a general election is on the horizon politicians are tempted to inject new cash and new programmes into the system to create some minor economic miracle with the hope that the electorate will be lulled into a sense of false confidence. But even when an election is not imminent, politicians are in constant danger of this temptation.

The third temptation that Jesus confronted was to be the imperial Messiah that Lawrence accused Christians of believing in. This might be the temptation to become a despot who uses his power to quash all opposition so that he can be the sole ruler of the world, or it might be the power of the party in a communist state. In his refusal to worship the Devil, Jesus rejected all forms of authoritarianism, whether the single dictator or the grey reign of the proletariat. Jesus rejects the force of the rich and he also rejects the force of the poor. He will be subservient to neither because he knows that only by serving God can the kingdom come. Again, this temptation confronts all of us at every level of our lives. Not many of us are tempted to be Hitlers, though some of us may be little Hitlers in our own sphere, but many of us are tempted to be benevolent dictators thinking we know best what others need. Jesus, in overcoming this temptation, refused even to be the benevolent dictator.

One of the reasons for the failure of the inner-city public housing dream was that it was invented by planners and politicians and given to the people whether they wanted it or not. It was good to want to rid our cities of decaying and inadequate housing, but for architects and designers to foist their ideals on others was asking for trouble. Much of that housing is now either hard to let or demolished, and rightly so. The sad fact remains that one cannnot easily compensate the families who had to live through the rise and fall of this dream.

Our Lord's three temptations give us some crucial insights into the nature of power and its possible misuse. We must not attempt to buy people, we must not attempt to use our power to twist arms, and we must not assume the role of dictator either individually or collectively. Having rejected these three forms of messiahship, the rest of the New Testament goes on to tell that Jesus adopted the radical alternative of the suffering messiahship that exercises power by way of a cross.

In making this choice Jesus not only set the pattern for his own unique work. He also set an example for his followers. Christians use power by way of weakness, by taking up their cross daily. Paradoxically, in very weakness lies strength, and in being broken for the sake of others the kingdom comes. We must learn to use power not to gain our lives but to let them go. This is the true use of power which alone can transform individuals, families, the social order and the whole of creation.

In Revelation 5 the same truth is expressed in symbolic

terms. The question is asked: 'Who is worthy to open the scroll of history?' John begins to weep because no one on earth or heaven is found. But the reply comes back: 'Weep not; lo, the Lion of the tribe of Judah, the Root of David, has conquered, so that he can open the scroll and its seven seals' (Rev 5:5). Then John 'saw a Lamb standing as though it had been slain' (Rev 5:6).

The imperial Messiah, the Lion, has become the suffering servant, the Lamb. What John does here is to take one of the traditional Jewish images of the Messiah, the Lion, and give it a new and, at a deep level, an opposite meaning. Such an interpretation is, I think, justified when we consider the drama as it develops in this chapter.

In verse 5 the titles of Lion and Root of David are used for the Messiah, but what John actually sees, as recorded in the very next verse, is the Lamb bearing the marks of slaughter. If John had simply wanted to suggest that Lion and Lamb were two aspects of the nature of the Messiah then he could have used a compound image similar to those he uses elsewhere (eg Rev 4:6–8). The fact that there is a single image implies that John is contrasting Lion and Lamb and taking us to the heart of the matter. This is reinforced by the drama of the Lamb taking the scroll from him who sits on the throne. In the Old Testament a variety of images are used for the Messiah. What John does here is to stress the centrality of one of them, namely the Lamb. He does so for the same reason that Jesus in his earthly life stressed the attributes of service and poverty. Like the Jews, all of us have a tendency to want salvation by imperial power rather than by death and resurrection.

John's imagery teaches us that the Messiah rules not by imperial strength but by a life laid down. It is only this Jesus who can open the scroll, the scroll which represents the world and its history. Jesus alone shall reign because he is the only one who knows how to reign by being a servant. The challenge to us when we use power — any sort of power — is, do we use it as a lion or a lamb? The only legitimate form of power is lamb power.

Just imagine how industrial relations would be transformed in this country if lamb-power was used instead of lion-power. Many of our industrial disputes are characterised by each side using more and more aggression, more and more lion power, until they eventually degenerate into the pitched battles that we see on our TV screens. Both sides need to learn to resist the temptation as Christ did. Nor is it valid for one side in the conflict to demand that the other side be docile as lambs. Such a demand is nothing but a subtle form of lion power, and the oft-repeated slogan 'the right of management to manage' reveals an attitude which comes dangerously close to such lion power.

One of the difficulties with lamb-power is knowing what it looks like in concrete human situations. Lion power has the advantage here because it means gaining the upper hand and forcing people into submission. Perhaps one example of lamb power is the attempt by some trade unions to work towards no-strike agreements. Obviously, if no-strike agreements are insisted upon by management, then this is just naked lion power, but if trade unionists are willing to give up certain rights in exchange for a greater say in the running of a company for the mutual benefit of all, then a simple form of lamb power is involved. Alternatively, some firms have introduced worker participation in management by giving rights to representatives of the workforce to sit on councils and boards. Sometimes this is just cosmetic, but when it is genuine, simple lamb power is being displayed. The us/them situation is potentially trans-formed into an authentic community of interest. The reason that I describe such developments as simple lamb power is to register the fact that such agreements are, in their turn, being transformed into lion power as soon as one side begins to use them as threats to beat the other with. Lamb power is, in a fallen world, always corruptible, but when it is not corrupted, social relationships begin to bear fruit in unimagined ways.

One of the characteristics of lion power is that it distorts the biblical image of the Lamb. In order for lion power to work it requires that lambs should quietly obey all instructions and simply conform. Lambs are not supposed to make any protest whatever: they should bear their lot with fortitude and silence. But the biblical picture of the Lamb is *not* of someone who wouldn't say boo to a goose. The biblical picture of the Lamb is of someone who courageously lays down his life for others. It is precisely because of his protest that his life is on the line. The lamb will protest by a call for justice, the lamb will protest by reinstating a social outcast, the lamb may even protest by his silence, but his witness will be clear and it will be dangerous.

In his stand for non-violent protest, the figure of Ghandi comes to the fore in the twentieth century. No human being is perfect, and there was a certain naïvety in his political philosophy, but his approach did enshrine something of the lamb power approach.

In the Book of Revelation John uses the title 'martyr' or 'witness' of Jesus himself and also of his followers who literally lay down their lives for his sake. Not all Christians are called to make this ultimate sacrifice, but the loyalty of those Christians who are called to do it is an indication of the devotion of all. Because our Lord could ask any of us to go to this level of loyalty, our commitment to him is a martyrdom commitment.

When John uses this word 'martyr' he uses it with two meanings. First, a martyr is someone who literally lays down his life for others. Second, a martyr is someone who stands as a true witness in a courtroom, he is one who tells the truth even though it involves great personal cost. Jesus bore witness to the truth at his trial where he said to Pilate, 'Every one who is of the truth hears my voice' (Jn 18:37). When Jesus had to stand for the truth he had no personal security to fall back on, he had no personal fortune, he had no power to wield behind the scenes. His was not a case of a golden handshake and being asked to resign quietly. Rather he stood naked and

vulnerable, his only strength coming from the knowledge that
God is King.

Perhaps once, perhaps twice in our lives, we will be called on
to witness to the truth in this naked kind of way. It may be a
situation where standing for truth means loss of job, loss of
reputation, loss of financial security, loss of family and loss of
friends. But thank God that even when such major crises come
we will never be called to stand as naked as did our Lord. We
will always have his example and his faith to sustain us. The fact
that he stood the test and became the faithful witness means that
we need not fear. We will certainly have to face the crisis
because he has promised that the crisis will come, but we will
not have to stand alone.

But martyrdom commitment is also something for the
smaller crises of everyday life. Being the faithful witness and
using power in our daily lives in a lamb-like way is a
characteristic of the follower of Christ. It is knowing how to
face each situation with the strong weakness of Christ himself.
It is learning to pray the prayer of Christ, 'Not my will, but
thine, be done' (Lk 22:42).

CHAPTER FOUR

THE FAILURE OF SUCCESS

THE BOOK OF REVELATION is both an apocalyptic and a
prophetic book. It is apocalyptic because it tells of the end
of this age and the dawn of a new age: it is prophetic because it
points to the meaning of history here and now.

When I was vicar of a church in Liverpool we did a series of
Bible studies on Revelation. We took a different chapter every
week, and each week a certain member of my congregation was
disappointed because the end of the world hadn't come. But the
first twenty chapters of Revelation are about the meaning of our
history here and now. It is only in the final chapters that the end
comes. When John talks at the beginning of the book about the
'time being near', he has in mind not the end of the world but
the forthcoming crisis of persecution in the church. During
John's lifetime the Roman emperors had made more and more
claims about their divinity. John could see the time rapidly
coming when it would be impossible to render to Caesar the
things of Caesar and to God the things of God — Christians
would soon have to choose one or the other.

Revelation speaks to us today about this same kind of crisis in
two ways. First, there are some Christians who are literally in
the same position as the early Christians of Asia. There are
countries in our modern world where Christians have to decide

between obedience to the state and obedience to the gospel, and where they are often imprisoned or exiled just as John was. Second, there are many more Christians in our world who do not live under such repressive regimes but who confront the same crisis at a deeper level. Those of us who live in the affluent West are dangerously near to a sell-out to the values of consumerism and materialism. We often deny that we are near such a crisis by using our Lord's words about giving taxes to Caesar as an excuse for keeping spiritual values and material values separate. But Christ came to be Lord of all and we should subject all to his kingship. His words about taxes must therefore be interpreted in this light.

John was probably sent to the Isle of Patmos for refusing to offer incense to the Emperor Domitian who claimed the title 'God'. From our vantage point in the twentieth century, the issue appears purely religious and also black and white. The fact is that it was neither. It was not black and white because we know from contemporary literature that many people who did not really believe in the emperor-god myth were prepared to offer the incense because they regarded such acts as being part of the ordinary civic and ceremonial aspect of life. Its main function was a form of pledging public allegiance to the state and, for this reason, people were prepared to forego their private religious scruples even if they had any. Such a lax attitude towards religious beliefs may be hard for us to imagine, but we need to remember that most people in the Roman world were polytheists and to add one more minor god to their pantheon would not have caused them any great difficulty. No doubt many Christians were tempted to take such an approach. Right from the start the church had a high regard for the state and this commitment could easily have been used by Christians as a reason for treating the incense as a purely civic gesture.

The civic nature of the incense ceremony also shows that it was not a purely religious matter. In the ancient world to refuse to worship the particular gods of a conquering people could be seen as treason. States were identified to some extent with their religious cults and so to refuse to join in the worship could be taken as a form of political disloyalty. The Roman state was, as far as we can tell, fairly liberal when it came to the religions of conquered peoples. They even allowed the Jews religious freedom, although the Jewish religion must have seemed strange to them. But the emperor-god claim was used as a rallying point to unite the empire through loyalty to the emperor, especially in times of unrest. The religious ceremony of the incense was, therefore, a political act as well as a religious one.

This put Christians such as John in a very difficult position. They could not deny their Lord and yet they wanted to be loyal citizens. It was through this dilemma that John began to see that any state which deifies its emperors must be on the slippery slope which ends up in totalitarianism. The parallels today would include those Christians who live in communist countries where official atheism is built into the system or in countries such as South Africa which claims a Christian basis but shows a totalitarian attitude towards its black and coloured population. It would also be right to include, as I hinted earlier, the more subtle questions faced by Christians living in cultures where the prevailing values are not those endorsed by the gospel. Cultures as well as states can make totalitarian claims that need to be resisted.

For Christians in the first century and for us today the moral, social and political questions that we face are subtle and complex. This does not mean that we should give up in despair. Rather it means that we should work towards an open and serious debate which accepts that sincere Christians will some-times take very different points of view. In conducting this debate we need to establish some ground rules if we are to be faithful to John's approach in Revelation. First, because John describes Jesus as the faithful martyr, we must not cling to political, social or moral points of view simply to defend our own comfort or lifestyle. The gospel calls us to take up our cross daily in his service and this means that we must be wary of defending ideas that are convenient to us and our families. Secondly, like John, we will not hide behind the subtlety or complexity of the issue and throw in our lot with whatever establishments we belong to. Because it is easier to go along with our own political party, trade union, or even our own churches, we must be prepared to make a critical stand where necessary. This can be very painful for all concerned, but our faithfulness to God must be ranked above all other loyalties. Thirdly, we must remember that when we have arrived at our decision we must not force it upon others. In the next chapter we will see how such a principle fits in with John's symbol of Christ — namely, the Lamb. We must be prepared to allow others the freedom to come to their own views before God, otherwise we stoop to the Devil's methods of force and coercion. Even if we are proved right in the end, this never justifies us in the use of totalitarian methods.

A fourth overarching principle is also suggested by the order of Revelation. After the initial vision in chapter 1 comes the section concerning Christ's words of judgement upon the seven churches. Before he judges the world he judges the church. Therefore when Christians assert the moral, social and political values for which they stand, they can never point the finger at the world without first being willing to sit under the judgement of God themselves. DH Lawrence interpreted Revelation as being about God's judgement on the world and his acquittal of the Christians, but such a view is in direct contradiction to the sequence of events in the book.

The biblical principle is that judgement always begins at home, and for this reason I want to look in detail at Christ's words to the church of Laodicea. The greatest totalitarianism that those of us who live in the West are tempted to succumb to is the materialism and consumerism of our success-orientated culture. If we fail to see the negative aspects of the culture in which we live, we cannot hope to be true salt and light in the world.

Laodicea was a rich and successful banking city, and the church there was wealthy, well attended and well respected. Perhaps the Christians of Laodicea were tempted to believe that God's kingdom had already come. Perhaps creation had reached its fulfilment, for this rich and powerful city with its rich and powerful church combined all the joys of splendid living with the blessing of a thriving community. But by describing himself as 'the beginning of God's creation' (Rev 3:14), Christ reminds the Laodiceans that the kingdom is not about being rich and successful; it is about producing men and women like Christ. The kingdom can only come when human beings take on the maturity of Christ, and that maturity includes his vulnerability and weakness. The whole creation waits with eager longing not for material success and well-attended churches, but for the revealing of the suffering servants, the sons of God.

Material success had actually made the Laodiceans lukewarm. The water supply in their city came along an ingenious five-mile long aqueduct from a fresh spring outside. There was a pure supply of clean water in abundance, but when the water arrived in the city it was lukewarm. The water and the aqueduct underline the inadequacy of material success alone. The best engineering skills could only bring water so tepid that one wanted to spit it out.

Christ's word to the Christians in Laodicea is that they have taken over the values of the city lock, stock and barrel. It is right that Christians should value local culture wherever they are because that is part of what reverence for the created order means. It is also right that Christians should learn to understand culture so that they can be all things to all men. But it is a betrayal of the gospel when Christians sell their birthright for the sake of a particular culture. A hidden danger lurks within cultures of success, such as those at Laodicea and also modern

Europe and the United States. It is all too easy for gospel values to play second fiddle to cultural ones.

To this successful city with its successful church, Jesus delivers three severe reprimands which strike at the very heart of its pride. First, the Laodiceans are told to buy gold refined by Christ. How shameful this must have been to a city famed as the banking centre of the region! Christ declares that all riches must be dedicated to him before they can truly serve the purpose for which they were created. Like the Laodiceans, we Christians in the wealthy West need to dedicate all our wealth to God. This will mean a critical look at all our income and investments both private and public, and it will also mean learning to put our own needs, and those of our families, in the perspective of a world torn by poverty. Secondly, the Laodiceans are told to buy white robes to hide their nakedness. What an embarrassment for a city famed for its clothing trade! And the sting in the tail is that Laodicea was famed for the production of raven-black cloth. Here Jesus reminds them and us that all our material possessions are utterly inadequate if we are spiritually naked. The lie of materialism is that in the end it gives us nothing. We may pretend to ourselves that all we do is simply provide for ourselves and our families to the best of our ability. But Jesus reveals the sham — our motives come dangerously near to selfishness and pride.

Finally, the Laodiceans are told to ask for eye-salve to cure their blindness. How ironic for a city with a medical school famed for its Phrygian eye-powder! They cannot see beyond their outward success and therefore they cannot see their true need of Christ. The values on which their city is built and which their church reflects are hollow and without substance. We, like the Laodiceans, need to buy from Christ the eye-salve which will allow us to see the poverty of the values which underlie our church and community.

In these three reprimands Jesus takes, one by one, the church's and the city's strengths and reveals them as weaknesses. As is so often the case, the values of the kingdom turn the values of the world upside down. It is not that money, material possessions or success are wrong in themselves; rather it is the use to which they are put. The biblical witness as a whole gives us two main tests for our wealth. The Dives test asks, does your wealth serve the poor and enable them to flourish as well as yourselves? (Lk 16:19–31). The Abraham test asks, if God called you to give up what you value most in this world, would you do it? (Gen 22:1–12). If we can answer 'Yes' to both of these questions then we have two signs that we are putting God's kingdom first. However, we must allow these questions to search us deeply. It is no good answering the Dives question positively if I simply give a small donation to charity when someone puts an envelope through my door. I must ask the question of all my wealth and all the benefits that accrue from it. Christians should, therefore, take an interest in investment policy and the way in which the politics of wealth operate in society.

The issues that face the Laodicean church are also crucial for the church in the West today. As we have seen, many of them are related to the problems of success. It has to be said that the church is often more pure and godly when its back is to the wall and its members are in poverty. However, we must also recognise that success is of God for the right flourishing of creation and human beings is part of the goodness given to the world by its Maker. Christians need to know how to handle success without falling into the Laodicean trap. The real challenge for the church today is the challenge posed by the political, social and economic system within which we live. Too often this system robs the poor to pay the rich.

As Christians we need to develop radical initiatives if we are to avoid the Laodicean mistake. Such initiatives will include alternative trading systems such as those developed by Traid-craft where the emphasis is on just trading relationships rather than simply on profit. In this way the lower-paid workers in the

Third World and in our own society will not be exploited. With
the credit boom, alternative banking systems may need to be
devised to protect the weakest and most vulnerable in our
society from excessive interest rates. Ways need to be found to
incorporate the Old Testament principle of zero interest rates
for the poor (Lev 25:36). The credit unions that are springing up
in some of our inner cities are small examples of this, but the
Old Testament points us to a more widespread review of
financial structures. The nineteenth century saw the generation
of a large number of philanthropic trusts and institutions.
During the course of the twentieth century the responsibility
for health, education and welfare has been shouldered more and
more by the state. But in the 1980s some reappraisal is going on
about the balance between state funding and private charitable
trusts. It is no bad thing that such a reappraisal is happening, but
Christians need to stand firm on two biblical principles. First,
the responsibility for the poor, the weak, the sick and the
elderly is a community responsibility that private charity can
assist but should not be expected to shoulder. Secondly, all
social systems such as education, banking and health care must
ensure just and equitable treatment for disadvantaged groups.

The *Faith in the City* report produced by the Church of
England has highlighted the plight of those living in our urban
areas. Because modern societies tend to concentrate the socially
disadvantaged in inner-city areas and urban housing developments the issues raised in the report represent a challenge to all
who live within those societies, whether they are inner-city
dwellers themselves or not. The fate of the inner cities becomes
a litmus test of our social concern because of the way in which
the disadvantaged are forced to live in such areas. If, as
Christians, we refuse to heed the prophetic challenge of such a
report then we are in danger of coming under the same
condemnation as the church in Laodicea. This church was
meant to be a lampstand, a shining light in its community, but
it was so overshadowed by the surrounding culture that it made

no impact at all. If we do not stand for justice in our society, Christ will remove our lampstands.

In many of our inner-city areas Christ has already removed the lampstands of the churches of the traditional denominations. Many such churches have moved to greener pastures in the suburbs, often having commuter congregations which disguise the fact that there is no local Christian life. Thankfully our Lord has given lampstands to new churches, often black-led ones, in inner-city areas so that light may continue to shine. But at the end of the day, Christ's will is that churches should not simply represent one social group or culture. Church growth theory may tell us that people like to become Christians within the safety of their own culture, but any church which is going to proclaim the gospel must be multicultural in its vision. Even the good things about our human cultures can be used to keep others at arms' length, but the gospel breaks down all barriers that separate.

All the New Testament letters to churches are to churches in a certain place or city. This fact enshrines a very deep truth about the mission of the church. Wherever a church is, it is called to be a witness to the whole of that society. If Christ were to write to us, therefore, he would want to write to the angel of the church in Britain. Sadly, he could not so write if the churches in this country only minister to one section of the community.

When I worked in Liverpool two ordinary working-class lads were converted at the youth club. Our church was a working-class church, but very much the traditional, respectable and hard-working variety. These two lads were of a newer generation and they were on the dole. In some ways they fitted well in the church, but in other deeper ways they did not — there was a subtle culture gap.

The crisis came when they wanted to do something about the poor children who lived in their block of flats. They saw these children going about in tatty clothes with worn-out shoes on their feet, and naturally they wanted to help. They asked if they could set up a 'Scruffy Kids' Fund' in the church as a start. Their request was heard at the PCC meeting. They spoke clearly and passionately about setting up such a fund, but they were given the bureaucratic reply — we can't do anything this year since we already give 10 per cent of our income away; you will have to try again for next year's budget.

In one sense this reply was good and sound, but in another sense it was blind. Here were two young people eager to do something practical about their faith, and we put them off. Annual budgets, forward planning — these things were not part of their culture. Their response to our reply was to give up their new-found faith, at least as far as the church was concerned. They saw immediate need on the one hand and comfortable Christians on the other and they drew their own conclusions. When we lost the confidence of these two young people none of us noticed what a crisis the church was passing through. To most of us it just seemed a fifteen-minute item on an already crowded PCC agenda, but underneath was a very deep crisis. Had we kept the confidence of those two young Christians their zeal was such that many more conversions would have occurred and the church would have made a real breakthrough. We failed this challenge, but even more worrying was the fact that so few of us even noticed the significance of the challenge in the first place.

The church in the West is facing a similar challenge but on a monumental scale. Will we as denominations and congregations face the challenge of the poor? The trouble is that so few Christians even notice the challenge. We are so preoccupied with maintaining our own lifestyle and church structures that we do not hear the knock of the Lord. This is not the gentle Jesus meek and mild feebly tapping at the door; this is the Jesus on whom all history depends hammering with both fists at the city gate.

However, the knock of the Lord is not a demanding,

judgemental knock. The God of Revelation is not a God who is just waiting to catch his people out and thrust their guilt into their faces. He is the God of grace who wants to come in and dine with us. He knows that only by the power of his grace working in our lives and communities can our motives and our lives be renewed. He needs only one person within to hear his knock. If anyone opens the door he will come in with grace and fellowship to renew both the individual's heart and the entire community.

CHAPTER FIVE

FOR THEIRS IS THE KINGDOM

O F THE SEVEN CHURCHES to whom John is commanded to write in the Book of Revelation only two, Smyrna and Philadelphia, are left without criticism. It may surprise us to discover that both these congregations are described as struggling and barely managing to exist. The church at Smyrna is 'weak' and the church at Philadelphia has 'but little power', yet the Lord has uncritical praise for them.

When Jesus, in the Sermon on the Mount, says that the kingdom belongs to those who are poor in spirit, he really means it. The culture in which we live tends to stress the opposite and our natural tendency is, therefore, to praise and honour the successful and the strong. 'Initiative', 'drive', 'get up and go' and 'enterprise' are the buzz words, and respect seems to be reserved for those who have climbed the ladder and made it to the top. We are also tempted to take these values into our church life by looking for the signs of God's kingdom exclusively among those churches that are thriving, growing and expanding. But our Lord clearly warns against such a mistake when he declares that it is the weak and powerless churches of Smyrna and Philadelphia that are authentic.

The implication of this is that today we ought to look for the signs of the kingdom not just where churches seem to be thriving but also where they are struggling and finding it hard to make ends meet. Indeed, there is something very special about such churches because they are forced by their circumstances to rely more on the power of God than on any human success. We glimpse something about the heart of the matter when we realise that the values of the gospel turn upside down all the shallow notions of value and success that we imbibe from our culture. To say this is not to suggest that Jesus or John saw any glory in failure or weakness for its own sake. The message is rather that our human vulnerability is the very thing that keeps us open to God and that when we succumb to the false values of our culture we are in danger of leaving God out of our lives.

The letter to the church at Philadelphia actually kept me going as vicar of a small and struggling inner-city church in Liverpool because the biblical description seemed to fit us to a tee. I remember attending conferences and training days led by 'successful' evangelists and pastors who told us of packed churches and well-pastored flocks. These events left me feeling very guilty about the smallness of our work, and it took a great deal of spiritual courage, which did not come easily, to believe the message to the Philadelphians rather than the message of success.

In Jesus' teaching about the kingdom and in his words to Smyrna and Philadelphia there is something more than a simple questioning of the success ethic. There is actually a positive evaluation of weakness and poverty from the point of view of the kingdom. The truth about the poverty of the Smyrnans was that they were in fact rich, and the truth about the powerless Philadelphians was that Christ had set before them an open door of opportunity.

Something of this paradox can be glimpsed in today's debate about deprived regions, both urban and rural, and weak, struggling churches in our urban priority areas. This debate tends to assume that resources should be transferred from those who are advantaged to those who are deprived and that that is the end of the matter. Rich suburban churches should help struggling inner-city churches with money, manpower and expertise, but the Bible is quite clear that the weak and struggling churches also have important contributions to make to the life of the whole church precisely because they find themselves so straitened. The whole church needs to learn that these tiny broken congregations are the true resources.

The rich may have money and manpower to give, but the poor have the kingdom to share. The testimonies that are coming out of these urban priority area churches are for the refreshment and inspiration of the whole. Rural deprivation often remains hidden because numerically it bears no comparison with its urban counterpart and because some of the indicators used to measure urban deprivation, such as the presence of ethnic minorities, are not present. Nevertheless, rural communities and struggling rural churches have their own poverties from which we can learn.

The underlying reasons for contrast between our human values and those of the kingdom become clear when we look more closely at the church in Smyrna. The city of Smyrna was one of Rome's oldest allies and as such it won her special favour. The Smyrnans were shrewd — they knew which side their bread was buttered — so they vied with other cities in Asia Minor for the title of the first city of Asia. It is notable that the title given to Christ in this letter is 'the first and the last'. This is a reminder that although we may win the earthly race for the favour of others, something deeper is going on where the picture is almost the reverse. Real power and approval only come from God. Outwardly we may be successful, but if we win our lives at the expense of our souls then the race is lost at the more fundamental level. Jesus' declaration that 'whoever would save his life will lose it' (Lk 9:24) is a flat contradiction to the values of our success-orientated culture.

It is interesting to speculate on the poverty of Christians living in Smyrna. Specific reference is made to the role of the Jews in the letter to the church in Smyrna, and we know from the rest of the New Testament and other sources that they often instigated persecutions against Christians.

Perhaps there was a kind of pecking order in Roman society. The Roman citizen came first, those in the provinces came second, and so on. The Jews had only a low foothold in the social order and, being tolerated but not loved, they could be ordered out of the cities at a moment's notice. The Christians found themselves in an even more precarious situation as they occupied a position in society below the Jews. As so often happens in pecking orders, it is not so much the people at the top who persecute the people at the bottom, but the people just above them on the social ladder. Power and conflict operate within these pecking orders, and this could well be one of the reasons why it was the Jews who instigated the persecution of Christians in Smyrna as elsewhere. Certainly, much scholarly research suggests that the majority of Christians belonged to the lower orders of society, but even those who, like Paul, possessed full Roman citizenship or high social position (Romans 16:23 tells us that Erastus was city treasurer of Corinth) could be accused of anti-Roman activities by virtue of their allegiance to Christ. But whatever the reason, the letter to the church at Smyrna makes it quite explicit that it was the Jews who slandered the Christians.

Christ's judgement on the Jews of Smyrna in Revelation is that by the exercise of their power in the pecking order they have lost their birthright and the right to their name and have inherited the new name of Satan, the accuser and slanderer of God's people. Whenever we use power in this way we come under the same judgement. In our success-oriented culture it is all too easy to tread on other people to gain our own success, but when we succumb to that we earn the name of Satan. It is important to remember that it is the Lord himself who names the Jews as the synagogue of Satan, and it is he alone who can make such a designation. As a Christian I may react very strongly indeed when I hear someone who has never been unemployed condemning all those out of work as lazy lay-abouts, but I must not retaliate and call that person by the name of Satan because if I do this I am merely playing his game of condemnation. No, it is the Lord who designates the name of Satan and those with ears to hear will know the truth without using it as a weapon.

Although we may not ourselves slander other people with the name of Satan, it is very important to know who our accusers are. As an inner-city vicar it took me a long time to learn this lesson and my guilt went deep, making me both a worse human being and a worse pastor. What happened was that clergy and members of other churches that were more flourishing than ours would, by subtle insinuation, imply that we were somehow being unfaithful or too stick in the mud. Criticism also came from some who joined our church for a short while but found progress too slow for them. Such critical accusations gained in force because they were often only hinted at. The effect of this was that guilt began to build up inside me and, because guilt is such a negative force when it comes to motivation, I became increasingly tired and depressed. It took me some time to understand just what was going on. As I began to realise that my fatigue and lack of motivation had their roots in these accusations, I found release and new peace. Knowing that the work of Christ on the cross had freed me from their power gave me new energy and vision.

The process by which accusation leads to guilt and then apathy is not confined to the life of the church. It also has a political and social dimension. Recent research into the psychology and behaviour of young unemployed people suggests that something very similar is going on. Society, particularly through the popular press, gives young people the impression that it is their own laziness or lack of motivation that is to blame for their inability to get a job. This pervasive accusation then produces deep guilt in the young people concerned. The fact that in some parts of our society there are only ten jobs available for every fifty school-leavers does not seem to alter this self-blame effect. In the end this guilt leads to apathy and lack of motivation. What such young people need to learn is to resist society's accusations and stop blaming themselves. In coming to realise that such accusations are false, the self-defeating cycle of guilt and apathy is broken. Thus, much of the demoralisation that comes with unemployment could be averted if those who are unemployed could be empowered to resist accusation. From a Christian standpoint we know that such empowerment only comes when we accept the victory of Christ over Satan.

The Smyrnans are warned that they would soon face persecution. In the mercy of God it would be short, but it would still be real enough. Some Christians would be thrown into prison on remand before their trial and, no doubt, some would only come out of prison to face the death penalty. But they would be able to face physical death because they knew that they had been declared immune to the second death. On earth they were accused and slandered by the Jews, but these accusations held no real power because God did not accuse them and because they found approval in his eyes. 'Who shall bring any charge against God's elect? It is God who justifies: who is to condemn?' (Rom 8:33–34). These words of Paul contain an aweful judgement on those who accuse the poor or weak in any context.

The story of the church at Smyrna does not end with the Book of Revelation. We know from later letters and documents that the church there survived for many years. We also know it suffered sporadic persecutions right up to AD 156 when their bishop, Polycarp, was martyred by being burnt at the stake. Even as late as 156 the Jews still seem to have been the ringleaders and those who gloated most at the persecution of the believers. The story of the martyrdom of Polycarp, which was written down by the Christians at Smyrna shortly after his death, takes us on a stage in our consideration of power.

The story starts with a man named Quintus who, in an act of bravado together with some others, gave himself up to the authorities. Later when he saw the wild animals that were going to be set upon him his fear, together with the powerful persuasion of the governor, made him recant his Christian profession and take the oath of allegiance to the state. Polycarp heard of this but was not afraid. He wanted to stay in the city but the local Christians persuaded him to leave for a place of safety, so he moved to a quiet farm just outside. By this time the authorities were looking for him. They made a search of the area but found nothing so they took two boys from a nearby farm and one of them confessed under torture to knowing the whereabouts of the bishop. At this stage Polycarp could have been smuggled away to another place of safety but he refused, deciding to stay where he was and to spend his last hours in prayer.

In the evening the chief of police, ironically named Herod, came on horseback to take his prisoner. The old man went willingly. On the way into the city the chief of police tried to persuade Polycarp not to make a stand. 'What harm is there in saying "Caesar is Lord" and burning the incense and saving yourself?' But Polycarp was not to be persuaded. They soon arrived at the arena where, once again, the attempt was made to dissuade him by the governor. 'Take the oath and I will let you go. Revile Christ.' Polycarp replied with words of great humility and courage: 'For eighty-six years I have been his slave, and he has done me no wrong; how can I now blaspheme my King who has saved me?' Yet still the governor tried to dissuade him. Eventually, when they could see that nothing would change his mind, they burned Polycarp at the stake.

Apart from the great courage of Polycarp there are a number of lessons about the nature of power that this story reveals. On the surface it is a story about the Roman state which had the power to outlaw or liquidate any opposition to its rule, and which was prepared to use the whole force of the law and its police to achieve this. However, the truth is that real power did not lie with the mighty Roman state but with a frail old man of eighty-six who had never wielded any weapon in his life. The quiet strength of this defenceless old man was the strength that eventually conquered the Roman Empire. But this old man's power is not just displayed in the hindsight of this victory; there are marks of it within the story itself.

Any establishment is always afraid of dissent and will go to any lengths to silence it. However, the preference is always to convert its dissenters to its own point of view. There may have been compassionate motives on the part of the chief of police and the governor when they tried to dissuade Polycarp, but their fundamental motive was fear. They knew that this old man, weak as he was, represented a threat to their established way of life. We are always in danger of falling prey to the fear of the establishments to which we belong but, like Polycarp, we must resist the temptation to conform.

The greatest weapon in the armoury of certain establishments is that of atheism. It seems strange to our ears that the early Christians were charged with atheism, yet one of the slogans that Polycarp was asked to give assent to was 'kill the atheists'. In a society where polytheism and idol worship was practised and where the emperors claimed divine status, the Christians must have presented a stark contrast. They believed in an invisible God who called them away from allegiance to these so-called deities. In this way they were like the Jews, but unlike the Jews they did not belong to one nation and did not have one heritage. The God the Jews worshipped could be easily understood as the God *of* the Jews. In one way the Romans could relate to the Jews as they had a clearly defined territory and cultural heritage. But there was no way the Christians' God could be understood in national or establishment terms. They were therefore branded as atheists because their claims seemed to strike at the heart of the establishment's power. In saying no to the Roman gods they were saying no to the state. This was reinforced in that Christians did not do military service, nor did they offer themselves as magistrates.

When the Archbishop of Canterbury preached at the thanksgiving service after the Falklands War, he refused to glory in victory and chose rather to thank God for its end and to urge prayer for the injured and fallen on both sides. His low-key approach upset some who felt that he ought to have struck a much more victorious note. But to have done so would have been to succumb to the temptation to believe that God is on our side only. When, as in this case, a church leader refuses to bestow divine approval on the actions of the state, he must be prepared for a critical response. He is, in a sense, saying, 'I do not believe in your gods.' It was such reservations that made the early Christians refuse to burn incense to Caesar and this is why they were open to the charge of atheism.

The figure of Quintus in the Polycarp story does, however, lead us to qualify the notion of dissent. It seems that Quintus' action was one of bravado. We also know from other sources that some early Christians gloried in martyrdom and, unlike Quintus, went through with it. The church realised that this was not altogether healthy and so came to teach that it was wrong for Christians to give themselves up and seek persecution deliberately. I would emphasise here that to seek to glory in any form of dissent should come under the same condemnation. It is a misuse of the power of weakness, and is just as insidious as the force of any establishment. The quiet humility of Polycarp, not seeking to run away but not seeking notoriety either, is the Christian model of dissent. He quietly stands for the truth, not parading his loyalty to Christ but simply acknowledging Christ's loyalty to him.

When Polycarp confessed this loyalty in the arena, the crowds shouted for a lion to be set upon him. He was in fact burned at the stake and it was the power of the Lamb which enabled him to stay in the flames without being nailed to it.

The Beasts

The Enemy Within

Revelation chapter 13
Romans chapter 13

CHAPTER SIX

I WANT TO RULE THE WORLD

W E HAVE SEEN that our Lord's praises for the churches of Smyrna and Philadelphia, and his severe warnings to the outwardly successful churches such as those at Laodicea, are a penetrating critique of all success-oriented cultures. However, this is not a celebration of failure, nor does it imply that our hopes, dreams and ambitions are unChristian and sinful. A false type of Christian spirituality has tended to suggest just this. It has argued that the teaching of Christ on self-denial means an end to all personal ambitions and goals, and that his teaching on servanthood means a stamping down of all personal dreams and desires. The influence of this spirituality on the corporate and political sphere is to urge the sacrifice of all individual ambition and drive for the general and public good, and to try to prevent the growth of a person or group beyond the average. This false interpretation of Christianity does not do justice to the teaching of the Book of Revelation. Weakness and vulnerability are celebrated there, not for their own sake but because they point to the power and kingdom of God. This understanding of weakness and servanthood gives us a truly Christian understanding of ambition and desire for success.

I vividly remember sitting in a pub one evening in my parish in Liverpool where we had gathered for a celebration and farewell party for one of our eighteen-year-olds who was going to university the next day. This was a very special occasion for us because few young people from our part of Liverpool ever succeeded in getting a place at university. After a few drinks this lad blurted out, 'I want to rule the world.' In that one phrase he had summed up all his hopes and ambitions for the future. At that moment he felt that he could take on the world and win. This was more than just the excitement of the moment and it was certainly much more than one working-class lad from a deprived inner-city area wanting to make it safely into the middle classes. He sensed the infinite opening up of his horizons as the world lay before him with all its opportunities. Within him he felt that he had the energy of soul to master it. There was nothing malicious or selfish in his desire because as he saw the world at that moment it was big enough for everyone to fulfil their dreams.

To have desires, hopes, ideals and ambitions, and to long for their fulfilment, is part of what it means to be human. We all reach for the moon, we all desire to be gods. And to want to be a god is, in fact, a God-given desire. We will see later how this desire can turn to violence and destruction, but we should remember that essentially it is a good and right desire. Indeed, when we cease to long for the moon we begin to write our own epitaph, for to stifle or deny this desire within us leads to bitterness, the withering of creative energy, and a kind of spiritual death.

In the parable of the prodigal son, the younger son claims his half of the inheritance and goes off to make his fortune in the world. He leaves behind his father and his family who are hurt at their rejection and at the selfishness they see in him. Among the pigs the prodigal begins to come to his senses. Eventually he returns home to a father who rejoices that his dead son is now alive again. Seflishness is a form of death, and when we seek to fulfil our own dreams by exploiting and treading on others we not only kill them but also ourselves. But even within the younger son's selfishness there are seeds of hope that eventually bring him back home. In the older brother who never left home but gave his all for his family without complaining, a worse form of destruction is at work. It is the destruction brought about by a false denial of his own hopes and dreams, of years of resenting others' opportunities. The younger son is able to respond to his father's love, but the older son cannot do so because of his deeply negative attitude towards his own needs and dreams.

The same is true not only of individuals but also communities and nations. The Western world greatly fears that communist regimes sap the individual of his initiative; they cut down the giants of the human race to the level of the average.

The price of realising the laudable dream of equality is the sacrifice of all individual ambition, drive and hope. From our position in the West it is difficult to know whether this deep fear of communist regimes is justified. It would take a great deal of research to prove it one way or the other. However, we can state categorically that if any community or nation deprives its members of their hopes, dreams and ambitions then it has become bestial. For John, the Beast of Revelation was the Roman state with its emperor.

Although we need to recognise that to want to rule the world, to long for the impossible, to desire the moon is all part of our God-given nature and should not be denied, we must acknowledge that it is dangerous. When we try to fulfil our desires we can wreak havoc for ourselves and others, bringing all our hopes and dreams tumbling down around our ears. We can destroy the world. This is the background to Revelation 13. When emperors such as Caligula, Nero and Domitian indulged this God-given desire they turned the Roman state into the Beast. Instead of seeing their desire for the moon as God-given and seeking fulfilment for it within his kingdom, they deified their desire and so the natural became beastly.

Revelation 13, alluding to the Book of Daniel, describes a

beast with seven heads and ten horns. It is like a leopard but has bear's feet and a lion's mouth. The seven heads are the seven Roman emperors and the diadems mean that the state claims that its ruler is king of kings. The seven heads bear blasphemous names like the name on the coinage of the Roman Empire. Claudius, Vespasian and Titus all had the name *divus* on their coins, and in the East that word was translated *theos*, meaning 'God' or 'divine'. Nero appeared on his coins as 'God' and Domitian demanded the title *Dominus et Deus*', 'Lord and God'. When we seek to fulfil our own dreams and ambitions without regard for others we actually demand the same title, for we are asking them to pay homage to us and our ideals. All ideals, all hopes, all ambitions must be subject to the rule of God.

At the present moment many Western-type economies are experiencing something like a renaissance of the ideals of free enterprise. Those who support such a renewal affirm that people should be given as much free choice as possible to pursue their own hopes and dreams and that it is the job of governments to create a climate where this can happen. Restraints on trading and on company and personal taxation should be kept to a minimum in order to lessen the load on the entrepreneur. Only in such a free-market economy, it is argued, can the rags-to-riches dream come true. But the weakness of this vision is its failure to recognise that in the kingdom of this world my desire for my moon means that you can't have yours. Such a naked appeal to self-interest, even to enlightened self-interest, also fails to acknowledge that in a fallen world freedom for some means bondage for others. It is for this reason that any unmodified, unredeemed notion of free enterprise, must be identified with the Beast of Revelation, just as much as the unredeemed notion of equality.

Our God-given need for fulfilment becomes beastly when we give it the elevated status of an unquestionable right. Even to take the first step along this path is to enter that wide road which leads to destruction. Unfettered, free enterprise does allow some to make it to the top, to be free to pursue their ideals and ambitions, but the awful consequence is that it also means that others will have their hopes and dreams trodden upon. The deprived urban areas, especially those of our large inner cities, are full of people who have been ground down by the freedom of others. It is a totally false myth to believe that anyone and everyone can make it out of the ghetto. This myth only gains its strength because those of us who are 'successful' need to believe it for our own comfort's sake. The myth is, itself, one of the most powerful instruments of oppression.

Until 1979, all post-war governments had acted to offset the increases in inequality generated by the labour market through increased welfare spending. It was also deemed to be of the highest priority to keep unemployment as low as possible. With the Thatcher administration, both of these objectives were subordinated to controlling inflation and reducing the role of the state in the market. It was argued that only by such measures could the economy regenerate itself and bring a new prosperity to all. But the results of such a change in direction have not, at least so far, produced the promised results. It is true that those whose earnings are above the average have reaped many benefits, but those whose incomes fall within the bottom third have seen none of them. The promise that wealth would trickle down from top to bottom has not materialised. In fact, the gap between the top and the bottom continues to widen each year.

The government's own figures (*Social Trends*, HMSO, 1988) show that in terms of original household income (income before tax and cash benefits) the bottom fifth of households fell from 0.8% of the total to 0.3% of the total from 1976 to 1985, while the top fifth of households increased their share from 44.4 to 49.2%. The figures for the final income of households (after income tax, cash benefits and indirect taxation) are, of course, not so stark but they nevertheless reveal the same process. In 1976, the bottom fifth of households received 7.4% of the total and this reduced to 6.7% in 1985 while that of the top fifth went up from 37.9 to 40.2%. With the 1988 budget changes reducing the basic rate of tax by two points, such inequalities can only get worse.

Nor is there any real hope for change in this process in the next few years. For a large number of households (the bottom 10%) there exists a poverty trap whereby real increases in wages will not result in real increases in household income. Because of the way in which social security benefit (now income support) is calculated, wage earners in households who earn between £70 and £140 per week gross will have money stopped from benefit, almost pound for pound, until they reach beyond the £140 figure. Surprising as it may seem, many people do earn well below this figure and so the poverty trap is very real.

Thankfully, unemployment levels are now falling (although it is difficult to make comparisons with past figures because of changes in the way in which they are calculated and because so many young people are now on government schemes). But there will still be over two million unemployed for the foreseeable future and the economic recovery that has taken place tends to favour certain areas of the country. The so-called North/South divide is very real when levels of unemployment in the North still remain high. Without some form of governmental redirection of wealth to the North, it is hard to see how market forces alone can stop the process whereby the regions become impoverished in comparison with the South-east. For the regions and for the bottom third of the population in economic terms, the prospect remains bleak despite the fact that the top two-thirds have benefited greatly from the policies of the present government. The figures do not support the trickle-down argument. In fact the gap seems to be widening. We must therefore beware of the doctrine of free enterprise unless it actually begins to live up to its promise for all sections of the population.

But the beastly does not only come in the form of exaggerated cultures of free enterprise. The ideal of equality, if simplistically applied, may also lead to repression because it can be used to crush all that is unique about us. Like the notion of freedom, the political idea of equality needs to be seen in the light of the gospel. The Old Testament tempers the freedom of the individual with its special appeal on behalf of the poor and the sojourner and with the vision of corporate community responsibility. The New Testament gives us the ideal of the body where each member is given equal respect in order to contribute their varied skills and gifts. These are but some of the fundamental scriptural insights which, when they are acted upon, prevent the state from becoming bestial.

The Roman emperors who claimed to be divine and the Roman state which became the Beast are a warning to any individual or nation which even begins to exalt its own ideals, doctrines or ambitions over others. Although John says in Revelation that the number of the Beast could be understood by anyone in his day, scholars today are not agreed on its meaning. Most think that the number is an example of gematria — letters standing for numbers. There is, for example, some graffiti in Pompeii which reads: 'I love the girl whose name is *phi mu epsilon*.' In other words, 545. But in gematria, two names can have the same number. 666 may refer to the Emperor Nero. The name 'Nero Caesar' certainly adds up to 666, but only if we transliterate it from Hebrew. A better suggestion is the Emperor Domitian because on coins of the period he had the title *Autokrator Kaisar Dometianos Sebastos Germanikos* which adds up to 666.

In his play *Caligula* Albert Camus is probably nearer the mark when he depicts the Emperor Caligula as wanting the moon. The moon represents the desire for the impossible, the desire to rule the world felt by my young parishioner on the eve of his university career. But in the play this desire leads Caligula to pursue his freedom at the expense of others. The desire corrupts itself and, in trying to make the impossible possible,

Caligula begins to destroy himself and others. If he is a god, he argues, why should he be the servant of fate? Most of us when we desire our moons come up against the force of circumstances in just the same way. But Caligula's response is to outdo fate. Why wait for famine to strike when, being a god, I can bring famine tomorrow? He therefore closes the state grain stores and the people begin to starve. Again, he argues, why should my freedom be limited by your freedom? He therefore demands absolute loyalty from his court to the point of asking them to die voluntarily for him.

In all this he is seeking light and freedom, but all he discovers is gathering gloom, destruction and madness. Caligula has become the archetype of all who put their own freedom on a pedestal. In his final speech, as he looks at himself in a mirror, he says:

> The Impossible! I've searched for it at the confines of the world, in the secret places of my heart. I've stretched out my hands see, I stretch out my hands, but it's always you I find, you only confronting me, and I've come to hate you. I've chosen a wrong path that leads to nothing. My freedom isn't the right one. . . . Oh, how oppressive is this darkness.

Caligula has discovered the horror of all who put their own freedom above that of others. He has discovered that in the kingdom of this world my moon becomes not only your bondage but my own bondage. It is only when we abandon the kingdom of this world for the kingdom of God that I can have my moon and you can have yours. It is only when we take the terrifying step of giving up all our ideals, hopes, dreams and ambitions into the hands of God that we discover our true life and true freedom. The words of our Lord, 'For what does it profit a man if he gains the whole world and loses or forfeits himself' (Lk 9:25) are not only a critique of personal hopes and ambitions, but also of our so-called success culture.

The first step in submitting all our ideals to God is listening to some of the fundamental insights of Scripture about community and using them as a critique of the values of our own societies. Christians have a fundamental prophetic role in any society in which they find themselves because they have the task of setting godly ideals and visions before their fellow men and women. The second step is worship. It is only as we actively learn to adore and glorify the living God that social justice becomes possible. This is why it is so fitting that Revelation has such a strong emphasis on worship, for it is only as we fall down before God and offer him all our ideals that we can see things in the right perspective. Social justice must always, therefore, be seen within the context of worship and evangelism. The church's worship on earth is crucial in the fight for justice and it is evangelism which calls people to put their faith in Christ alone.

CHAPTER SEVEN

INTEGRITY IS NOT ENOUGH

IT IS NOT DIFFICULT to see that someone who pursues his own ambitions in a purely selfish way will limit the ambitions of others and destroy them. What is more difficult to recognise is that the same dangers still exist when our hopes and dreams have a moral character of their own. A communist country can use the laudable ideal of community to browbeat and enslave its citizens. A capitalist country can so enshrine the notion of freedom into its system that a massive poverty trap can virtually imprison whole sections of the community. I can destroy other people with my selfish ambition, but I can also destroy people with worthy, even Christian ideals.

William Golding tells the story of a dean whose dream was to build a spire on top of the tower of his ancient cathedral. For the dean this was far more than a purely architectural enterprise; he wanted the spire to point people to heaven and therefore to prayer. Ultimately the spire was a symbol that would point people to the kingdom of God. From a Christian point of view he couldn't have had a more praiseworthy aim. For the dean this was far more than simply a private ambition. Rather it was a dream, a vision, to be undertaken in obedience to God.

As he contemplated the building of the spire he felt the warming presence of the angel of God and, with this assurance, he began the realisation of his dream. But as he explained his plan to others nothing but objections were raised. The chapter (the members of the governing council of the cathedral) were against the plan because of its prohibitive cost and the risk to life and limb. The master mason explained that the existing tower had weak foundations that would never take the strain of the added weight. But the dean saw all these as materialistic concerns which belied a lack of faith. For him faith was that which calls us to do the impossible and therefore such arguments were overruled.

The building work was started and, as stone was laid upon stone, the foundations began to crack. The strain of the work on the clergy and masons began to tell. Men died, men turned to drink, men were psychologically destroyed, but still the dean called them to go higher. As the story progresses, the dean's warming and reassuring sense of the presence of the angel becomes a sense of a demon driving him on. The tower is eventually completed, by the mercy of God, but everyone including the dean is emotionally, physically and spiritually destroyed in the process. Perhaps one could say that the dean's vision was a mistake in the first place and that his guiding angel was a demon all along, but such an interpretation is inadequate. Rather, it was that as he called for more and more loyalty, more and more worship of his dream, it turned into a nightmare.

Golding's story shows in a most frightening way that even the very highest ideals can be used to crush other people. There is nothing selfish about the dean's proposals. Indeed his motives seem to be beyond question, for his whole desire is to call people to faith and trust in a God who can do the impossible. One might say that this is the highest ambition, the highest vision, that any human being can ever have. And yet, in the way in which the story unfolds, we can see that even angels, even the message of the kingdom of God, can be turned into an instrument of torture. When this happens the holy has become bestial.

The immediate application of this story is within the

Christian community itself. I know of a church where the pastor likes to think of himself as the teaching elder. In one sense he does not consider himself to be king of the castle, and most of the work of the church and its management is left to other elders and lay people. But the pastor does believe that he has the trump card. Because of his training and experience in interpreting the Bible he believes that whenever there is a question for the church to address that is more than a purely practical one, then his role as interpreter of the word of God must be seen as central. More than this, anyone who does not regard his interpretation of the word as final must be put under discipline.

Like Golding's dean, this pastor's motives are entirely pure. He is not a megalomaniac who is deviously using his role to get his own plans approved. He is totally sincere in wanting to do God's will. Nevertheless, he ends up using a worthy ideal to silence all opposition. The final outcome is that those who disagree with him are excommunicated from that Christian fellowship.

We need to realise that this will always be the final outcome when we regard our own visions and ideals as inviolable. This is a subtle form of self-deification because we turn loyalty to ourselves and our visions into loyalty to God. Although we may start off with sincere motives and moral dreams we inevitably end up, like Golding's dean, demanding more and more loyalty, more and more obedience. It is this loyalty-demand syndrome which poisons the morality of the original vision and turns it into a vicious weapon. The process at work here is none other than that which led the Roman emperors to take on the title *Dominus et Deus*. Whenever we begin to demand absolute loyalty from others we are, in effect, demanding to be treated as God. No human being should ever expect such loyalty or give it, not even in embryo, for that is to worship the Beast.

Once or twice in my ministry I have felt that my superiors

have been close to demanding this sort of loyalty and, being a fairly weak person, I have been tempted to give it. But summoning up all my courage, I have refused to comply. It has only been by remembering the charge that we should worship God alone that I have managed not to succumb. My experience is that such tests come in very subtle ways. It is not so much the big issues on which we feel we have to take a stand, but rather the hidden dynamics of our relationships which so easily slide into this form of emperor worship.

Many of the students that I help train for ministry in the Church of England are also perplexed by this issue of loyalty. Should they be loyal to the clergy under whom they serve as assistants, or should they be true to their own convictions? The question is not easily answered, especially when it is posed in such a general way, but I do find myself worried by a lot of senior clergy whose immediate response is to say, 'What I look for first of all in a curate is loyalty.' In one way there is nothing suspect in such a statement, but it is sometimes spoken in such a tone that one suspects a desire for emperor worship. Revelation 13 is quite clear — we should only give conditional loyalty to one another. If we do not heed this teaching then we let loose the demon who can kill even with good and wholesome dreams.

The demonisation of good dreams coupled with the loyalty syndrome operate in all spheres of human relationships. At the time of writing, both this country and the USA have right-wing governments that affirm the principles of free enterprise and individual freedom. Those who have opposing political views often attack such governments on the grounds that their goals are fundamentally immoral. The argument is that any government which favours the rich against the poor must be immoral to its core. The implication is that if only politicians like Margaret Thatcher or Ronald Reagan were honest they would acknowledge that their outward show of moral integrity was mere icing, and that the truth of the matter was that they couldn't care less if the disadvantaged go to the wall.

However, it is precisely because such right-wing views are held with moral integrity that they become so dangerous, for any dream held with such integrity can blind people to what is going on before their eyes. The poor, the unemployed and the disadvantaged go to the wall because the vision is such a dazzling one. This is not, of course, a danger just for those politicians who affirm free enterprise; it is a danger that applies equally to the moral visions of the left. In a communist state it is all too easy to label those who do not fit in as dissidents and to banish them to labour camps or psychiatric institutions. To us this seems barbaric, but to those who are officials within the system the dream of an equal society can lead to blindness and hard-heartedness.

On a recent visit to the States I listened to a great deal of radio and television. Beneath the discussions of current affairs the message seemed to be that the United States is the greatest nation in the world and its mission is to save the world and keep it free. No one ever stated this explicitly, though a few came quite close. While such a high moral and salvific vision is worthy, it is also highly dangerous. Human beings commit atrocities in the name of truth and righteousness, as history only too clearly shows.

It is within family relationships, however, that the most subtle forms of emperor worship are encountered. Although in recent years there has been a revolt against the Victorian concept of the husband as the boss and the wife as the chattel, the issues of power, loyalty and worship are still a force to be reckoned with even in the most enlightened families. Sartre, the French philosopher, said that all relationships are fundamentally either sadism, masochism or indifference. Stated in this bald way his conclusion appears exaggerated and even perverse, but when we begin to think of the complex ways in which we dominate others and allow them to dominate us, we can see that it is a very perceptive analysis of the relationships between fallen men and women. Because we are fallen we tend to use other people, even our nearest and dearest, to fulfil our own desires. Our Lord himself was aware of these demands for worship within family relationships and he was forthright in his verdict: 'He who loves father or mother more than me is not worthy of me' (Mt 10:37). It is only when we begin to see our family loyalties in the context of the lordship of Christ that they can be freed from Sartre's terrible trinity. As a young Christian I had to face this head on because my own parents were very much against my wishes to train for ordination. I can remember many rows and arguments that turned on this very issue of loyalty. It was made more difficult because the Bible itself lays such heavy stress on our duty to our parents. But in the end I had to follow my calling in my own broken way.

The issue of dreams, hopes and moral integrity is closely related to our understanding of the Holy Spirit and his power in our lives. In Golding's novel the dean had a classic charismatic experience. He went ahead with his vision not because it was a worthwhile plan worked out by irrefutable logic, but because of his warming angel. Whenever he contemplated the vision he felt warmed by an angelic presence. He took this as divine confirmation of his dream to construct the spire. But such an understanding of the work of the Spirit is not fundamentally Christian.

The great promise of the New Covenant is that the Spirit is to be poured out on all. The new age is characterised not by sporadic visitations of the Spirit to isolated individuals but by God's activity in the whole community. The proclamation of the prophet Joel, taken up by Peter in Acts, is, 'I will pour out my Spirit upon all flesh' (Acts 2:17). Thus for any individual to claim an unquestionable vision from God which is independent of community testing is to make God's promise a lie. Such community testing will avail itself of the advice of those who have special gifts of spiritual discernment, and it will also take into account the advice of its leaders, but in the end it is the whole community that must make the decision. In his commentary on 1 Corinthians Barrett points out that the phrase 'when you are assembled' refers to the formal assembly of the church which, at the end of the day, must take corporate responsibility for spiritual judgements. Therefore, in overriding his colleagues, and even in overriding the practical advice given to him by his master mason, the dean failed to submit to the Spirit.

Another important truth hidden in Golding's story is the difference between dreams and visions on the one hand and concrete ambitions on the other. For any of our dreams to come to fulfilment they need to be translated into practical policies, strategies or goals, and it is in this practical translation that things can go sadly wrong. The dean's dream was to point people to God, and his practical strategy was to build a tower of stone that would enshrine this dream. The trouble was that though his dream was genuine, his concrete ambition to build a spire seemed to be nothing more than folly to others. From this we learn that there are always two stages to the testing of any vision. The first is the testing of the vision itself, the second is the testing of the concrete plan of action that is proposed. It may well be that one could endorse the former and not the latter or vice versa. Such a consideration is especially important in the political sphere because we often tend to justify particular policies by appealing to certain broad visions such as freedom of choice or community responsibility. What we need to do, however, is to address both the general vision and the particular policy in their own right.

The distinction between dreams and concrete ambitions also helps us to account for the deep lack of satisfaction that many people find in our materialistic and success-orientated culture. The dream is to make something of one's life without being dependent on others; to provide for one's family, to enjoy the good fruits of the earth, to find fulfilling and exciting relationships, and to have space to explore one's own creativity and uniqueness. Such dreams are right and good but all too often they are translated into inadequate and mistaken concrete ambitions. Bigger houses, faster cars, higher pay, financial security — these things cannot satisfy our deeper longings. Even our more subtle ambitions for fame or a happy family life can prove to be empty. Such dissatisfaction may tempt us to renounce our dreams in favour of some anti-materialistic religion, or we may simply become more materialistic by trying to forget our deeper selves and moving from one concrete ambition to another. But both these options are flawed. True fulfilment only comes when we submit both our dreams and our concrete ambitions to God. He may well endorse the longing but lead us to some better ambition which in the end proves more satisfying for us and for others. The trouble is that we are often so wedded to our particular ambitions that we cannot let them go.

Finally the question of integrity must be raised. Anyone can see that integrity coupled with a suspect or evil moral vision can be devastating. No doubt Hitler believed with total integrity in his vision for a new Germany and a new world, but with disastrous results. We have a temptation, however, to approve of the value of his integrity while denouncing what we see as his immoral vision. But such an analysis is only partial. From a Christian point of view we must also question the nature of integrity itself. The danger with integrity, especially with the integrity of a leader, is that it can lead to a form of self-worship that is tantamount to a belief in one's own divinity. If I put my integrity above that of others then I am in danger of declaring myself a god. Integrity can, all too easily, slide into self-justification and this is one of the themes of the Book of Job.

Job is an upright and godly man. We are told quite specifically that this is not just his own estimate of himself; it is the Lord who declares that there is no one on earth as faithful and good as Job. But as the book unfolds we see that it is Job's very integrity that mars his relationship with God. Thankfully Job does not give in to the false humility called for by his counsellors, but in his subsequent arguments with God he has to learn to come to the point where he puts all thought of his own integrity aside and simply bows in obedience to God. In the end Job comes to repent in dust and ashes. He is not repenting here for any wrong done except that of putting his own integrity outside the kingdom of God. Job learns the joy of justification by grace when he lets go of his own efforts at self-justification.

It may seem strange to us, but the truth is that we need to let go of our own integrity before the kingdom of God can come. I realise how dangerous such a doctrine is. We have come to believe that, almost by definition, the very last thing we must let go of is our own integrity. We fear that if we let go of this ultimate moral principle then moral chaos will ensue. This is indeed the case when we abandon our own moral integrity simply to fit in with other people. Our own moral integrity must remain intact when we live in human community. But at the deepest level of our relationship with God we must allow his integrity to come first. To put the point starkly, we either worship God or we worship ourselves. In the end there are only two kingdoms — the kingdom of God and the kingdom of the Beast.

CHAPTER EIGHT

LEFT WING/RIGHT WING

IT IS A PERPLEXING FACT that Christians of both left- and right-wing persuasions appeal to the Bible as giving justification for their views. The established churches such as the Church of England, which has had the reputation of being the Tory party at prayer, stress obedience to the state, while Marxist Christians in the Third World talk of civil disobedience and even revolution. Right-wing Christians tend to point to passages such as Romans 13 which talks of quiet and respectful servitude, whereas left-wing Christians appeal to the prophets of the Old Testament and to passages such as Revelation 13 where the note of protest is very marked. Both groups then go on to interpret the rest of Scripture in the light of their starting-point within a particular text. A careful look at Romans 13 and Revelation 13 will give us a way into this debate.

At first glance the teaching of Romans 13 seems quite clear. 'Let every person be subject to the governing authorities. For there is no authority except from God, and those that exist have been instituted by God. Therefore he who resists the authorities resists what God has appointed' (Rom 13:1–2). Traditionally such texts were used to condemn all forms of civil disorder and rebellion. Today right-wing Christians would use them to deny citizens the right of protest, the right to strike, and all forms of civil disobedience. The argument is strengthened because this text is not an isolated one in the New Testament. In other places Paul talks of children obeying their parents, slaves their masters and wives their husbands. Peter seems to apply this way of thinking to the general position of the Christian in society. He writes: 'Be subject for the Lord's sake to every human institution' (1 Pet 2:13). It seems that one cannot deny that Peter and Paul were totally establishment men. They both seem to support the classic view of Hobbes that without human institutions the life of man would be solitary, poor, nasty, brutish and short, and therefore total obedience to the state, even to the despotic state, is preferable to the chaos of civil rebellion which is the only realistic alternative. However, a closer look at Romans 13 will show a different picture. Several important points need to be made.

Underlying Paul and Peter's teaching on authority is the fundamental truth that all human authority is, at most, only secondary or derived. True authority belongs to God alone and in his wisdom and grace he gives some of that authority to man. And what God gives he can also take away. Because of this fundamental principle no state can call for unqualified obedience because to do so is to ask for that which belongs to God alone. I read in a commentary recently this summary of Paul's teaching: 'God himself is the fount of all authority, and those who exercise authority on earth do so by delegation from Him; therefore to disobey them is to disobey God.' This is actually a misinterpretation. Paul's actual words are: 'He who resists the authorities resists what God has appointed.' Far from identifying the state with God, which would be to deify the state and commit blasphemy, he actually stresses the difference between God and those whom he appoints. Paul's high view of the state does not conflict with the basic belief that God alone is God. In effect those who misinterpret Paul as identifying the state with God make the same mistake as Golding's dean. The call to heaven and to prayer can never be identified with the building of a spire. The one may represent the other but if they are thought of as one and the same then only totalitarianism can follow.

Another point about Paul's argument is that the notions of law and justice are intrinsic to it. Paul has in mind the state which rewards the good and holds the sword to the wrong-doer. He develops this theme quite explicitly, as does Peter. The civil order is given authority by God precisely because it has the function of bringing justice into the dealings of the human race. The question immediately arises, what of the state which tries to rule by flouting the principles of law and justice? Paul answers this in 2 Thessalonians in his treatment of the man of lawlessness.

He argues that the appearance of the man of lawlessness will usher in the great rebellion and the Lord Jesus will slay him. Paul's teaching here is remarkably like that of Revelation 13 because he sees this man of lawlessness exalting himself like the Beast, as an object of worship. More important for us, as we look at Romans 13, is Paul's idea that lawlessness and injustice are already at work and are only restrained by the mercy of God. Paul holds his high view of the state precisely because he sees the state as restraining lawlessness and standing for justice under God. Any state which calls for obedience without upholding godly justice cannot claim to uphold the ordinance of God. Augustine put it like this: 'Without justice what are kingdoms but great gangs of robbers?' Because of this fundamental concern with justice Christians are obedient to the state, but never in an absolute way. There will always be a tension between the two competing claims of duty to God and duty to the state.

So far we have seen that there are two limitations on the right of any state to call for our allegiance. The first limitation is that the authority of the state is at most secondary. The second is that there are limitations of justice on the power of the state. Romans 13 points to a third limitation, namely that the power of the state is only temporary. We now live in the night when the power of the state is authorised by God because it restrains lawlessness, but the day will come when a new order will dawn.

Before we begin to look at the implications of this for our modern situation, one more vital point needs to be made about Romans 13. When Paul instructs the Christians at Rome to be subject to the state, the word he uses is the Greek word *hupotassesthai*. This is not one of the ordinary Greek words meaning 'to obey'. If Paul had wished to instruct his readers to obey the state in the same way that he advised children to obey their parents, then he would have used one of these ordinary words. But he specifically chooses a different word when he talks of the responsibility of wives to husbands and citizens to the state. Occasionally, the idea of obedience is prominent (as when Paul uses the same word in Romans 8:7), but in the majority of the thirty cases in the New Testament, this is not the predominant thought. Ephesians 5:21 makes it clear that the overriding thought is one of voluntary and mutual obligation.

It means that the citizen has responsibilities towards the state but that the state also has responsibilities towards the citizen. This reciprocity includes our modern idea of civil rights. The citizen is the servant of the state but the state and its ministers are also the servant of the citizen. The relationship of *hypotasso* is broken when either party forgets to fulfil its obligations. Indeed, one could go further and assert that the state exists for the sole reason of serving.

A close look at Paul's argument and the meaning of the original Greek give us a very different picture from the traditional one. It is a picture that includes the principles of justice and rights for the citizen.

Recently I had to think through some of these issues when I decided to join a professional trade union. In recent years the belief that unions have too much power, especially political power, has grown. It has been argued that true prosperity can only come if unions are kept very firmly in their place and the law has been used to restrict the right to strike and picket. Although I do not wish to claim that trade unions have always used their power responsibly, I do feel that there is a great danger that we may swing too far in the other direction. Given the present mood of the country we could see the trade unions not only cut down to size but actually castrated. I put it as baldly as that because we have seen from our discussion of Romans 13 that justice and mutual rights are an essential part of good government. It is therefore very important for Christians to belong to organisations which play a part in the curtailing of the power of the state. Of course, careful discernment is necessary, but rather than being suspicious about institutions within our society such as trade unions and pressure groups, Christians should actually be at the forefront within them. These institutions, as well as the formal institutions of the state, are part of the total plan of God for society. Indeed such institutions, because they stand for the rights of the citizen, are part of those human powers ordained by God.

At first, when I began to think about joining a trade union, I struggled with a sense of disloyalty towards my employers in the college where I work. This seemed to be more of a problem for me in that I am a clergyman and the college for which I work is a Christian institution. But the more I thought about it the more I saw that it was being disloyal *not* to join such a union. At their best, trade unions have the function of restraining the tendency of every institution to take to itself more power than it ought. Trade unions are not adversarial; they are not against institutions. Rather they are part of God's system of checks and balances to remind all governing institutions that they must serve the cause of justice. Nor should the power of trade unions be restricted to purely local and narrowly 'trades' issues. It is perfectly proper, on a correct reading of Romans 13, to see institutions such as trade unions playing their part in restricting the power of central government in the political arena.

I want to emphasise this point because the current government policy on trade unions suggests that their role ought to be limited to trade disputes and the immediate needs of union members only. It is quite proper to require trade unions to ballot their members on the issue of the contribution of unions to political parties, but my interpretation of Romans 13 shows that there is nothing wrong in principle in trade unions affiliating themselves to particular political parties and movements. It is also proper to allow the health service unions the right of protest (this is different from the vexed question of the health unions going on strike) over government funding of the National Health Service. Such a protest is a political act because it seeks not only to change the pay and conditions of workers, but also more fundamental government policy.

The Acts of the Apostles throws light on the aspect of civil rights in Paul's teaching in Romans 13. After Paul had delivered a slave girl from the power of an evil spirit at Philippi, he and his companion Silas were dragged before the magistrates, beaten and imprisoned. After a miraculous earthquake and the conversion of the jailer the magistrates sent word next day that they should be released. However, Paul was not content with this, and so he decided that the magistrates should issue an apology because they were Roman citizens. Under Roman law citizens had clear rights and these rights had been infringed, and so Paul demanded an apology. Nor was Paul content when a messenger returned with the apology. He insisted that the magistrates should come in person to release them. This may sound to us as if Paul was full of his own importance, but when we view it in the light of Romans 13 we can see that Paul was insisting on his rights because they were part of the human institutions ordained by God.

A similar incident occurred when Paul made his defence before the crowds in Jerusalem. His speech was followed by uproar and arrest. The Roman centurion was just about to flog him when he claimed his rights as a Roman citizen. It is not too fanciful to imagine that the city which crucified Christ would have done the same to Paul had he not insisted on his civil rights. Paul's story has a further dimension. After spending much time in prison he invoked his right to trial before the emperor himself. Paul consistently relied on his rights before the law and used them to the full. The implication is that if we are to be faithful to Paul's teaching we must see full civil rights included in Romans 13.

Of course, Paul's reliance on his Roman citizenship and his appeal to Caesar all depended on rights that were laid down within the law of the state. We cannot appeal to Paul's experience to carry the argument forward into the area of protest and civil disobedience. But the story of Peter and John before the state authorities in Jerusalem does lead us into that area. After preaching openly in Jerusalem they were summoned before the council and strictly charged not to speak or teach in the name of Jesus. Their reply to the council is very important: 'Whether it is right in the sight of God to listen to you rather than to God, you must judge; for we cannot but speak of what we have seen and heard' (Acts 4:19–20). They then went on to what can only be called a planned programme of civil disobedience for which they were later arrested and thrown into prison. There is clear precedent here that when an issue is of such a fundamental nature then civil disobedience is the only proper course of action.

We have moved a very long way indeed from what I called the traditional interpretation of Romans 13. Before we move on to look at Revelation 13, two more implications of the traditional interpretation need to be exposed. Because Thomas Hobbes states the traditional view so clearly, I shall use his analysis. The underlying principle of Hobbes' discussion of the state is that we have to make a straight choice between a stable government with a totally subject people or chaos. Hobbes went one stage further by saying that either we have the chaos of the war of everyman against everyman or we have a state established by contract with a sovereign power which is not subject to the civil law.

It is easy to see why Hobbes was driven to this conclusion when we realise that he was writing in seventeenth-century England at the height of the civil war, but this does not justify his conclusion. I would argue that his principle of either/or is a fundamental mistake. The true either/or is that either we have a form of government which permits and even encourages civil rights and civil protest, or we have totalitarianism and the chaos that inevitably ensues. The very principle of absolute government which Hobbes thought was the only safeguard against chaos is, in fact, the very cause of chaos and revolution. The same truth expressed the other way round is that civil rights and civil disobedience are themselves the very guarantors of stability.

In an age like ours which fears chaos and the breakdown of law and order, we must take great care not to slip into an over-simplistic notion of social stability such as that held by Hobbes. If our only response to rising crime rates, inner-city riots, and violence on the picket line is increased spending on the police force and bigger prisons then we have already made a gross mistake, the upshot of which will be an ever-increasing spiral of social unrest on the one hand and heavier policing on the other. Instead we must espouse a broader notion of social stability based on the foundation of participation and community and a proper recognition of the meaning of civil disorder. Such a way forward would balance the proper enforcement of the law for the punishment of offendrs with a real commitment to tackle the root causes of social breakdown and disenchantment.

In British society at the present time getting this balance right is particularly important for those in their teenage years. Our courts seem to deal with growing numbers of people in this age bracket. Research, such as that done by Professor Frank

Coffield, suggests that the social contract between society and young people is at the point of breakdown. Heavier policing alone cannot solve such a problem. There must also be the social and political commitment to restore young people's confidence.

The second implication of Hobbes' view that we need to question is his treatment of religious dissent. Looking at Romans 13 he asks what we are to make of the Christian martyrs who should, according to Paul, have been loyal to the state. He goes on to argue that the only true martyrs are those who actually saw Christ in the flesh or those who have a specific calling and authorisation (presumably by the state) to preach and witness. All other martyrs are false martyrs. He suggests that for everyone else the Naaman principle should be invoked, namely, that we should worship God in secret and submit to the state, no matter what it demands, in public. In this way Hobbes narrows down to an absolute minimum any idea of Christian protest. In doing this Hobbes also distinguishes between the political and religious realms. What his view amounts to is that Christians and other religious groups should stay out of politics.

Our look at Romans 13 shows just how mistaken this view is. Paul's starting-point is that the authority of the state is secondary to that of God, and this means that conflict between obedience to God and obedience to the state is always possible. In addition, the principles of law and justice are intrinsic to Paul's understanding of government. Thus he stands in complete agreement with the prophetic tradition of the Old Testament where the prophets criticised the state when it fell short of the vision of justice which they believed was rooted in God himself. The prophets spoke out for justice not simply because Israel or Judah had broken their special covenant with God, but because justice was seen as a universal call as it is fundamental to the nature of God.

The prophetic tradition of the Old Testament is also the true background to Revelation 13 because, in addition to the prophetic stress on justice, there is also the prophetic belief in an impending crisis. The prophets foretold a crisis of judgement which would reveal the true nature of present-day realities. In a similar way, John looks at the world around him and sees the impending crisis of a Beast rising out of the sea and another Beast rising from the earth who call all men to worship them and be their slaves. With his eyes opened by God, John sees that the crisis is looming because he sees that men are beginning to worship the Beast. For John the Beast is the Roman state which has called for that which should be reserved for God alone — absolute loyalty, total obedience and worship.

Prophecy is rather like a negative transfiguration. When Jesus went up the mountain with Peter, James and John, he was transfigured before their eyes and revealed to them in all his glory. For this brief moment, and because of the coming crisis of the crucifixion, they were allowed to see Jesus as he really is. In a similar way, the prophet looks at the ordinary world around him and God gives him a glimpse of the stark reality of injustice and corruption. Those who are caught up with the day-to-day concerns of ordinary life are blind to these deep realities and fail to see the crisis ahead, but the prophet sees the crisis because his eyes have been opened by God to see to the very depths of things.

This understanding of prophecy helps us see why Romans 13 is so different to Revelation 13. I have already shown that the fundamental teaching of both texts is similar because they both rely on the prophetic understanding of law and justice. What makes them different is that they are words from God for two different ages. Romans 13 has the settled age in mind, whereas Revelation 13 has the age of crisis in mind. That this is a correct understanding of the difference is proved by Paul's words in 2 Thessalonians 2:8 where he sees the lawless one as being revealed sometime in the future. What Paul saw as a future event John saw as something at the very door and this is the reason for the difference in tone between Romans and Revelation. In Paul's own lifetime the Emperor Caligula had tried to set up his own statue in the Holy of Holies in Jerusalem but had been persuaded against it. In other words, the crisis of allegiance never really presented itself. But John saw that crisis as a growing reality ready at any moment to burst with all its fury onto the stage of history.

The confusion between an age of crisis and a settled age is well illustrated by the endorsement given to the Nazis by the established churches in Germany before World War II. No doubt Christians were misled by the increasing prosperity, falling unemployment and renewed confidence in the nation. Those Christians who supported the new regime gave these and other good reasons for their action. But the truth is that Nazism was fundamentally racist and the churches ought to have seen this embryonic evil that would later grow into the beast. Instead the vast majority of church leaders, both Protestant and Catholic, gave their support to the Nazis in 1933 and failed to protest against the persecution of the Jews. A small confessing church did arise, and some protested at the cost of their lives, but there was a serious failure in the established churches. Working within the system for change is appropriate in the situation indicated in Romans 13, but not when a crisis is looming.

Hitler's Germany also raises another disturbing question in that Germany was, and remained, a 'Christian' country. It is all too easy for Christians today to see the beast in communist countries where there is an explicit denial of God, but as a prophetic people we should be able to look beneath the superficial to the underlying reality and see the beast in nominally Christian countries. The great prophet Amos proclaimed God's judgement on nations that were overtly heathen, but he also proclaimed that same judgement on the 'godly' nations of Judah and Israel as well. The prophet sees beyond the labels to the underlying truth.

Is our age a settled age or is it an age of impending crisis? Are the states to which we belong already gestating the beast within or are the restraining institutions ordained by God doing their work? Are the institutions within which we are employed and within which we live our daily lives functioning within the limits set by God or are they becoming bestial? These are the crucial issues posed by Paul and John, and we need a prophetic vision to answer them.

CHAPTER NINE

NOT MY UTOPIA

HOW CAN WE KNOW whether we are in a Pauline or Johanine generation? Should we remain quiet or should we become refuseniks? It is only by listening to the voice of the prophets that we can decide such issues because a prophet perceives deeper truth beneath earthly realities. But how can we recognise the true prophet?

When I preached the series of sermons on which this book is based, some of my listeners called me a modern day prophet. Because I was addressing some of the issues in our community and the wider nation, and offering a critique, the word 'prophetic' seemed appropriate to describe what I was doing. But to describe everyone who offers a critique of present-day structures as a prophet is to stretch the word too far. And to call anyone who makes any form of protest against society a prophet is to debase the word altogether. One way to avoid this mistake and to understand the true nature of prophecy is to distinguish between a critic on the one hand and a prophet on the other.

In his own day DH Lawrence was called a prophet because he offered a systematic and radical critique of society. He saw around him a society ignorant of the depths of true life because it was harnessed to utilitarian values and the making of money.

Science and technology had been made subservient to human greed and the desire for dominance, and Lawrence believed that this had gone so far that man's very life was at stake. Life had been reduced to the purely mechanical, and England was dehumanised by the spread of an industrialism which threatened to destroy both humanity and nature. Modern industrial society had made everything ugly, even obscene. In his essay 'Nottingham and the Mining Countryside' written in 1929, Lawrence said:

> The great crime which the moneyed classes and promoters of industry committed in the palmy Victorian days was the condemning of the workers to ugliness, ugliness, ugliness: meanness and formless and ugly surroundings, ugly ideals, ugly religion, ugly hope, ugly love, ugly clothes, ugly furniture, ugly houses, ugly relationships between workers and employers. The human soul needs actual beauty even more than bread.

Beauty could not flourish because society had become a machine-worshipping society, turning everything into mechanical gratification. In his stand against pornography Lawrence showed how sexuality had been reduced to the mechanical gratification of desire. Sexuality should be warm, loving and tender, full of beauty, life and spontaneity. To reduce it to the mechanical or imprison it within Victorian moral constraints is to dehumanise it and drain it dry of life. This is why Lawrence saw the prevailing moral attitudes to sex as really anti moral. Purporting to raise sexuality to a lofty ideal, they actually debased it, denying its very beauty and sanctity.

World War I was, for Lawrence, a gigantic exposé of all these false values. It revealed them for what they were: obscene, violent and totally destructive. The only solution was to look for other more human values and this search eventually led him to the long-vanished civilisation of the Etruscans. These people were the inhabitants of Italy before the Romans, and little was

known about them in Lawrence's day. He visited their tombs
and from the wall paintings and carvings he began to picture a
primitive and beautiful way of life which was everything that
his modern world denied.

In his book *Etruscan Places* Lawrence uses words such as
stillness, softness, warmth and beauty to describe the way of life
that he imagined. In the Etruscan tomb paintings he saw a
fullness of life and an abundant spontaneity that refreshed him.
These ancient people found gaiety and humour even in death.
In the naked figures, delicate, sensitive and full of the dance of
life, he saw not pornography but a truly moral sexuality. And
in this dance all were included, even slaves who appeared not in
the least bit menial but surging with vitality. From these tombs
Lawrence built up a picture of a life full of freedom, joy and
wholeness, a life of touch and communication, an aboriginal,
cosmic and pure world. The tragedy was that, like modern
industrial man, the Romans obliterated this pure way of life and
drained it dry. As Lawrence said, 'Rome with a big "R" wiped
them out.' He saw the Romans as a military, mechanical and
expansionist people who imposed their creeds, deeds and
cultural patterns on their subjects, thus destroying true life and
religion.

In describing this picture of the Etruscan way of life and its
overthrow by Rome, Lawrence offers us a profound critique of
modern society as he saw it. He pointed to his own ideal picture
to expose the failure of the world around him. This gives us one
definition of a critic as someone who uses an ideal picture, a
personal utopia, as the basis for a protest against the evils of the
world. The fact that Lawrence's utopia was based upon an
actual civilisation does not alter the fact that it is a comparison of
the ideal with the actual. In this sense Lawrence was a critic and
not a prophet, and what he was doing among the tombs of the
Etruscans gives us an insight into the difference between these
two activities.

In choosing the Etruscans Lawrence almost deliberately chose a people of whom little was known. True, there is a liveliness and naturalness in their paintings, and Lawrence's impressions do have some historical foundation, but he chose the Etruscans because he could let his imagination run riot without the constraints of too much historical evidence. Indeed, he disregards what little evidence was then available that the Etruscans were a brutal people. He also idealised the contrast between the purity of the Etruscans and the brutality of Rome. Lawrence's utopia was, then, a romanticised and idealised picture of an ancient people. He used this picture to sum up a lifetime's dissatisfaction with his own European world, and he used it in a very profound and deeply moving way. But idealisation is always a mark of the critic who basically contrasts the real world with his own utopia.

From my own experience I can give another example of the difference between a prophet and a critic. I was brought up in a working-class area in the Birmingham conurbation. I was born during the war, and I can just remember the rationing and shortages that lingered on after it. Life was materially difficult for most people in our community, but there was a cheerfulness and humour that seemed to make life full and worthwhile. My own mother was extremely thrifty, even miserly, but she did not lack exuberance, and there was always money to go out to the pub or to celebrate an important occasion. We saved on what some would call essentials, making do with the most basic of amenities, but despite this there was a richness and optimism about life which was very exciting to a child.

The stress was on the present and the immediate, and pleasure was a central part of life. Planning or saving for the future were never allowed to spoil chances for fun and enjoyment. There was also a sense of beauty and of making things special. We lived in a small house with my married sister, her husband and her daughter, but despite the cramped conditions we kept one room, the front room, special. We were only allowed to use it on rare occasions, but when we did the experience was almost mystical because everything was absolutely immaculate.

Life was always full of surprises. Relatives and friends just turned up — there were no diaries and appointments. We ourselves made no plans. If the day was fine we would decide there and then on a day out. Mother saved up and bought a second-hand car and we would often drive miles to visit relatives. Enthusiasm for the moment meant a fuller life; all the drudgery of planning was dispensed with. Even the rows and arguments, of which there were many, seemed to add to the excitement of life. We never knew when the next one would be. It would flare up in a moment, but it always seemed quickly forgotten despite the strength of passion expressed. There was a forgiveness of heart, as well as a fury.

People had a great sense of pride about life. I remember visiting the foundry where my father worked and being most impressed by the intricacy of his workmanship in what were very primitive conditions. I also remember the pride my mother took in our home. Nothing was of very great value, but everything was cleaned and polished and made bright with great care. Pride was evident, too, in people's character, a pride that prevented life from grinding them down. One of our best family stories is of my grandfather who took a day off work without permission to go to the races. As he stood at the bus-stop his boss passed him in his car, obviously noticing him but driving on. It turned out that he was also going to the races. The next day my grandfather went straight to the boss's office and handed in his resignation. He told his boss that he simply refused to work for someone who would drive past him at a bus-stop. The fact that this left the family virtually penniless until he got another job was less important than his pride.

All these qualities of life — the humour, the spontaneity, the celebration, the surprise, the pleasure and the pride — made for a non-materialistic and generous lifestyle. I left that world behind me when I went to a theological college to train for ministry in the Church of England. The training was not designed to turn people into middle-class professionals but that is what it did to me, at least externally.

My first appointment was in a working-class area of Liverpool, and to some extent I rediscovered my roots there. But my present job in my old college in a university setting brings me once again into a middle-class world which is a million miles away from my working-class origins. From the point of view of one whose social background is different, the values of my present world appear to contrast unfavourably with those of my childhood. Surprise is replaced by planning, celebration is replaced by the big show, pleasure is hedged about by a list of social graces, and spontaneity is replaced by calculation. Worst of all, people seem to spend a disproportionate amount of time worrying about their investments and gaining privilege for their children.

I have used my early experience to build up a picture of an ideal world which emphasises the moral short-comings of the world I now experience. In using my ideal in this way I am being a critic and not a prophet. The fact that I can see through the moral shallowness of my present world may seem prophetic, but actually it isn't because it comes from the simple contrast between this world and my own utopia. Like Lawrence's utopia, my ideal enables me to make a profound critique of modern middle-class values. Again, like his utopia, mine is based on fact. Values such as spontaneity and celebration were definitely part of the community within which I grew up. But as Lawrence idealised his Etruscans, I have also idealised my roots. In fact, the picture is not as pretty as I have painted it. Together with the surprise and the joy, there was also a lot that was brutal and destructive — certainly much that was restrictive and small minded. My idealisation makes me a critic with some useful insights to offer, but it does not make me a prophet. The prophet is more than a critic because his yardstick is not some utopia or set of values of his own, but the yard-stick of the nature of God and of his justice.

Both Old and New Testament prophets never give us more than glimpses of their 'new world'. Even the last two chapters of Revelation come far short of giving a clear picture of the new order, and so John too can properly be described as a prophet rather than a utopian.

The message of the true prophet always includes the call to repentance which entails putting everything under the rule of God. Sometimes biblical scholars contrast prophecy with law. They suggest, for example, that the Books of Exodus and Leviticus are different in nature to Books such as Isaiah and Jeremiah. But to draw this contrast is a mistake because the moral basis of both law and prophecy is the rule and justice of God. The fact that law and prophecy have the same moral basis also explains why they each in their own way point to the cross. Prophets, unlike utopians, know that the kingdom will not come by the kind of repentance that simply means turning over a new leaf or attempting to return to some idyllic set of values. The stakes are too high and the grip of evil too strong for this. It is only by the blood of the Lamb that the new creation can be inaugurated.

In his proclamation of the kingdom of God Jesus is himself the fulfilment of both the law and the prophets, He, too, sets his face against defining the kingdom and turning it into a particular political programme. Instead, he tells stories that illustrate the kingdom and reveal its true moral values in contrast with the values that he sees all around him. And it is precisely because the kingdom is not a political blueprint that it stands over against every culture and society. No nation and no human group, not even the church, can claim to be the kingdom because to do so involves a contradiction. Only the King himself, the Lamb that was slain, can be the King.

But if the kingdom cannot be defined, cannot be turned into a blueprint, then we appear to be left with the question with which we started this chapter — how can we recognise the true prophet? At one level we can answer this question but at another level it has to be left open. At the first level we can tell a true prophet because he stands in continuity with the biblical prophets as they draw our attention to the deep moral values of the kingdom. In particular, we must test to see whether the values he upholds are the same as those enshrined in the Beatitudes and parables. At a deeper level, however, there is no foolproof test for a true prophet. It will always be a case of 'he who has ears to hear, let him hear' and 'he who has eyes to see, let him see'. To suggest, as some do, that prophecy is a poor guide because we can never be sure if a prophet is genuine is to miss the central point. It is not that we test the prophet but rather that the prophet tests us and calls us to repentance, moral maturity and rebirth. The listener must always have the option of deciding that a prophet is not true, because any attempt to bypass that freedom is automatically to deny the kingdom.

In this way, kingdom values stand over against us and judge us. But the same truth has a more positive side, for as we seek to live by these kingdom values, our lives are liberated from all the old bondages. As we repent and turn to the Lord he gives us a new freedom which releases us from the worst aspects of our particular upbringing and culture. We remain part of the human family but our higher loyalties mean that we are not imprisoned by particular sets of human values.

CHAPTER TEN

ALL THAT GLITTERS

W E MUST NOW APPLY the understanding of biblical prophecy which was worked out in the last chapter to John's
treatment of the two Beasts in Revelation 13. In order to do this
we must remember the sequence of events that lead up to their
appearance. The seven seals and the seven trumpets of the early
chapters are like melodies and themes in a piece of music that
lead up to the crescendo of chapter 12, which is the birth of the
Messiah. Revelation is not a chronological book. Rather it is
like a symphony with three movements, the first of which ends
with the coronation of the Messiah and the casting out of Satan
from the heavenly court. He can no longer stand before God to
accuse the saints, and the words of Paul that we no longer have
any accuser are therefore fulfilled. We can now live the life of
the new age in which all barriers between God and man are
broken down. But the image of Satan being cast down to earth
is used by John to explain why those who live this new life have
so many crises, problems and persecutions in the human world.

Although he has been deprived of all authority in heaven,
Satan is not left without power. He comes to earth to consume
the faithful in a river of lies. Satan's work always depends on
lies and it is by his lies that he tempts us to worship the Beast.
Revelation 13 describes the Beast rising out of the sea, conjuring

up pictures of the primeval ocean, the abyss and the underworld which represent powers devoid of the kingship of God. Jewish tradition talked of two beasts, one called Leviathan which came up out of the sea, and the other Behemoth which came up from the land. For John, living in Asia, the Beast of Rome literally came out of the sea because it was the sea which brought the Roman galleys with their rulers and armies. Leviathan is not narrowly limited to the Roman state, but represents anything that elevates itself above the moral values of the kingdom. John therefore challenges every culture and political system to ask where its own Leviathan lies lurking.

Leviathan usually arises out of some natural or proper function of a political system which has somehow become cancerous and threatens the life of the whole. We have already seen that it is a proper function of the state to exercise authority and discipline over its citizens and, as long as this function is kept subject to just laws, then the body politic will work well. However, if this authority outstrips the bounds of justice, then tyranny rears its ugly head and will grow by leaps and bounds until it eventually deifies itself. This is the cancerous process that John saw at work in Rome and prophesied against.

Another social cancer is racism. It is necessary and right for human beings to live within distinctive cultures and even to have a measure of pride in them. Our cultures give us the experience of belonging to a community so necessary to our human development. But when this respect for culture begins to grow unchecked, it soon turns into racism and finally fascism. It was because National Socialism had, in one sense, natural and good roots that it took such a hold in pre-war Germany, but once it turned cancerous it could only destroy the nation.

Although there are strong elements of racism and tyranny in modern Western society, our own Leviathan threatens to rise up from elsewhere. The growth of the New Right, the Moral Majority and monetarism indicate where our particular cancer is likely to develop precisely because they draw our attention to some good and legitimate values in our society. The New Right stresses the value of individual freedom, and that as part of that freedom entrepreneurship should be allowed to flourish. Monetarism stresses access to free markets and the traditional values of capitalism. But Leviathan rises from the abyss as soon as individual freedom, entrepreneurship and the right to build up private capital go unrestrained. This particular form of social cancer is, of course, nothing new. The Old Testament, with its Year of Jubilee and severe restrictions on lending money at interest, shows that it needed to be kept in check even then. The beast that we are tempted to worship in the West today is materialism. It raises its ugly head whenever we believe Satan's lie that material possessions, status or success come before trust in God. Our natural and legitimate need for material fulfilment is turned into a god.

Blatant materialism is easy enough to spot. We see it daily on our TV screens when advertisers try to persuade us that we can buy happiness by the acquisition of more and more goods and services. These commercials gain their hold over us by promising, either explicitly or implicitly, that our basic human desire for security, fulfilment, friendship and sex can be purchased over the counter. Although we know that this 'promise' is one of Satan's oldest lies, it still takes a grip of our souls. Scripture has a high view of material possessions because they have all been created by a good God, But as soon as an individual or community falls prey to the lie of consumerism then Leviathan rises from the deep.

This naked form of materialism is powerful and destructive enough, but there is an even more deadly form that masquerades beneath an aesthetic appearance. The maxim that men need beauty more than bread, taken to its extreme, leads to a distortion of values. This maxim, when it is maintained by those who have both bread and beauty rightly sounds very hollow to those who have neither. It is therefore important to question whether it is right to pay ten million pounds for a painting in a society where some human beings are forced into homelessness. This does not imply that we should forget about art or consider it a luxury until more basic needs are met for everyone. Art and creativity are part of God's image in us and are therefore fundamental. In very poor societies, such as some of those in the Third World, it is art alone that makes people feel human because it raises them above the daily grind of poverty. Similarly, in my inner-city parish in Liverpool some of the young people who were unemployed and had left school with few qualifications discovered a new meaning in life by writing their own very moving poetry. The beast of aesthetic materialism rises not from art itself, but from materialistic values that are sometimes superimposed upon it.

It is significant that God calls Bezalel and by the gift of the Spirit bestows on him all the artistic skills necessary for work on the Tent of Meeting (Ex 31:2). This passage affirms two things about all art and craft — namely, that they are divine gifts of grace and that they are meant to be dedicated to the work of the kingdom. When human beings misdirect these divine gifts by using them to exploit others or simply to bring glory to man himself, God does not withdraw them. But their misuse means that their true purpose is not fulfilled.

The incident in the Gospels where a woman comes into the house of Simon the leper and lavishes the very expensive contents of a flask of pure nard on our Lord's head is often used in discussions about the funding of art. Some present objected strongly, including Judas (Jn 12:4), because they saw it as a waste of valuable resources that could have been used in the service of the poor. Jesus' response to this puritanical attitude is: 'You always have the poor with you, and whenever you will, you can do good to them' (Mk 14:7). It is absolutely right to see this statement as a rebuke by our Lord to those who by their penny-pinching attitude would reduce human life to a grey monotony. Liberality, profusion, generosity, beauty, colour and glory are attributes of God and he bestows these attributes on human beings. We can't wait until poverty is irradicated before we exercise the artistic gifts that God has bestowed on us, and it is legitimate and desirable that individuals and governments should resource the arts, even in the face of the competing needs of, say, health care and social security. Nevertheless some kind of balance needs to be struck. Our Lord's words are both a witness to the extravagance of God in creation and in man and also an indictment of the general lack of concern for the poor that the adversaries of the woman display. John's comment that Judas did not really care for the poor (Jn 12:6) reveals the true motivation for his objection.

Another aspect of aesthetic materialism is its imperialism. As soon as one community or society seeks to impose its artistic canons on others, then the true art of that subject community can only atrophy. Instead of discovering within itself its own creativity, it is overshadowed by the ready-made values of others and the true wonder and variety of art are missed. I believe that something like this has happened in Britain because of our class system. True working-class art has been over-shadowed by the artistic canons of the upper and middle classes. Thankfully, this is being realised by more people today, and the many new folk museums are a tribute to the often unrecognised art of the working classes. This is not to say that representatives of one culture ought not to call the attention of others to their own traditions and works of art. Rather it is making the distinction between a genuine sharing on the one hand and imposition on the other. Modern Britain gives us another case in point with the immigration that has taken place in recent years. We have the opportunity to see new artistic forms within these ethnic communities and to share our own with them. We must avoid at all costs the cultural imperialism so characteristic of aesthetic materialism.

In Tolstoy's novel *Resurrection* Nekhlyvdov struggles with the issue of aesthetic materialism as he ponders the values of

Russian society before the revolution. He sees the middle and upper classes living comfortable and cultured lives, blissfully unaware of those at the bottom of the social scale who had to eke out an existence as best they could. The truth finally dawns on him that the civilised values of his society were just a front.

> Everything was clear. It was clear that all the things which are commonly considered good and important are actually worthless or wicked, and all this glitter, all this luxury serve but to conceal old familiar crimes which not only go unpunished but rise triumphant, adorned with all the fascination the human imagination can devise.

Tolstoy tells us that Nekhlyvdov would rather not have come to this moment of illumination; he would have preferred to remain in comfortable ignorance. But once seen Leviathan cannot be ignored, for aesthetic materialism is actually frightening and more insidious than naked materialism.

Both these forms of materialism rely on the natural but false assumption that riches are a sign of social status. When we meet rich people we tend to react to them in a deferential way which implies that they have extra merit over and above the poor man. We tend to give them a greater esteem and invite them to take the highest seat in our house or hearts. If some benefactor gives a million pounds to a good cause then he is likely to be rewarded with some social honour, but if a poor man gives the price of a meal then society does not consider him for an award.

Another of Satan's oldest lies is to link riches and success with merit, and as soon as we begin to believe that lie Leviathan gains his life-blood. Long ago the Book of Job exposed the lie, but whole cultures still believe it and, even worse, Christians within these cultures still believe it. A person's merit, and therefore the respect that we ought to give them, comes not from riches or success but from the grace of God alone. Job's fortunes are certainly restored at the end of his ordeal, but there is no hint that he himself merits this restoration in any way. The message of the Book of Job is that God's grace is displayed both in his giving and in his taking away (Job 1:21). The Psalms also make it clear that it is often the wicked who prosper rather than the righteous, and Jesus himself says that God sends his rain both on the just and on the unjust (Mt 5:45).

The parable of Dives and Lazarus (Lk 16:19–31) shows that the Leviathan of materialism and self-interest can only survive when individuals and societies anaesthetise themselves against the poor. Jesus told this story in a society where charity and almsgiving were meant to be part of the social fabric and yet Dives was still impervious to the needs of the beggar at his gate. Dives was not an out-and-out selfish individual, as his concern for his brothers later in the story proves, but somehow or another he was blind to his social obligation. What caused his particular blindness we are not told, but it does point out the need for us to be vigilant against similar blindness.

Sometimes such blindness is created by the myths we use to distance ourselves from the poor. One such myth is the trickle-down theory of wealth which states that although the poor and the unemployed may suffer in the short term from monetarist policies they will eventually benefit because the wealth gene-rated by a slimmed down and more efficient industry will eventually perculate to the bottom of the economic pyramid. That such a view is a myth rather than a fact is shown by an examination of the British Victorian economy and the present economy of the USA. Victorian Britain had an economy which was strongly entrepreneurial and free-market and yet it also had extreme forms of poverty which wealth barely touched. The modern economy of the United States is also less socially determined than our own and yet there are large urban ghettos which wealth hardly ever reaches.

The Lazarus story itself shows that there is no automatic trickle down from the rich Dives to the poor Lazarus — it all depended upon Dives' personal goodwill. This is why in the Old Testament law provision for the poor is not left to natural economic mechanisms or to private goodwill. The Year of Jubilee (Lev 25:8), the release of slaves in the seventh year (Ex 21:2), the command to lend to the poor at nil interest and to provide the homeless with shelter (Lev 25:35) all demonstrate that any free enterprise economy must be regulated by social provision.

Another mechanism that materialistic societies use to anaesthetise themselves against the poor is to separate them from the rich. Dives had to pass Lazarus at his very gate, but we avoid this problem by separating the rich from the poor by suburbanisation. I remember showing some slides of my inner-city Liverpool parish when I first arrived to teach in a theological college. I had not chosen the slides to shock but merely to show the ordinary way of life we experienced in Liverpool. There were some students, however, who simply couldn't accept that such places still existed in England. When I quoted statistics to show that at least 20% of the nation was equally poor, I met with frank denial. My students couldn't face facts because they had lived all their lives in the cocoon of suburbia.

We also separate the rich from the poor by turning the poor into paper and numbers by bureaucracy. This particular mechanism is a favourite of both left and right wing. It eventually puts the poor on the other side of the reinforced plate-glass window of the dole office. The poor either get lost in the system because they cannot understand it, or they learn the rules and get branded as professional scroungers. Bureaucracy attempts to deal with people without love and therefore treats them as objects. Nekhlyvdov reflects:

> The whole trouble is that people think there are circumstances when one can deal with human beings without love, but no such circumstances ever exist. Inanimate objects may be dealt with without love: we may fell trees, bake bricks, hammer iron without love. But human beings cannot be handled without love, any more than bees can be handled without care. . . . If once we admit it, be it

for a single hour or in a single instance, that there can be anything more important than compassion for a fellow human being, then there is no crime against man that we cannot commit with an easy conscience.

In cultures with a long Christian tradition the substitution of charity for true compassion also anaesthetises the rich against the poor. Those lower down the social scale or those who have no way of supporting themselves and their families are looked upon as unfortunates to be patronised rather than equals who require justice. The charity mentality breeds a superior attitude on the part of the giver which is a sure sign of evil, and it is never long before charity devises pernicious systems which distinguish between the deserving and the undeserving poor. We must not fool ourselves — even in the name of doing good we can give birth to Leviathan.

CHAPTER ELEVEN

IN THE MARKET-PLACE

LIKE ALL EMPIRES the Roman Empire used local political systems to enforce and extend its power. It was not the Romans themselves, but the Asiarchs of Asia who administered the foreign empire in their own land. It is these local institutions that are represented by John's second Beast, Behemoth, that rises from the land. Such secondary institutions have to go to more extreme lengths to persuade their foreign rulers of their loyalty, often making them more evil than the parent institution. It is for this reason that worship of the Roman emperor was more highly developed in the Greek East than it was in the Latin homeland. Behemoth, therefore, represents all those who collaborate with a foreign power in order to maintain its rule.

We need to recognise that people collaborate for different reasons. Some Jews in Hitler's Germany collaborated out of plain fear. They knew that if they did not beat their fellow Jews into subjection then an even worse beating, or death itself, could result for them or their families. In *Nineteen Eighty-Four*, George Orwell reminds us of the frailty of our human nature and how plain fear can cause us to betray even those nearest and dearest to us. We all know just how tempting it is to fall down and worship Behemoth.

Sometimes more complex motives are at work in the

collaborator. No doubt like many local élites the Sadducees of our Lord's day collaborated with Rome in order to maintain their own power, position and privilege.

Others were probably willing to overlook Rome's darker side for the measure of peace and stability that they enjoyed. Perhaps they genuinely, even if naïvely, believed that Rome was some kind of hope for the nation. After all, Rome did permit their religious traditions to continue and even flourish.

The desire for hope, the refusal to believe the worst, and the ability to turn a blind eye to the looming darkness are some of the more hidden motives of the collaborator. It is these motives which, in addition to naked selfishness, help to explain why so many Christians collaborate with the materialism of our own culture.

Each Christmas my wife and I receive lots of circular letters from our Christian friends and we too have started to send out a standard letter to bring folk up to date with our news. One of the recurring themes in these letters and in Christmas conversations and sermons, is a lament about its commercialisation and slide into materialism. It is often said that the true meaning of the Messiah being born in a humble stable is lost amidst all the tinsel, glitter and spending. Such sentiments are of course just, but the danger with them is that we do not take heed of them ourselves. The amount of money we spend on cards and presents, many of which will never be used, is probably more than the family of someone who is unemployed has to live on for a whole month. We are not saved from materialism just because we are aware of the deeper meaning of Christmas. Rather we are judged by our own complicity with the values of this world.

Those of us who are reasonably comfortable materially need to take heed lest we fall prey to the materialism of the 'haves'. We must not imagine because we feel free from greed and desire for more that we are safe from danger. Instead we must reassess our possessions and bank balances to see how they can be properly dedicated to the King. I realise that in writing in this way I may give the impression that Christians are kill-joys who ought not to go in for big celebrations, but this is to miss the point. Celebration is fundamental to life itself and without it we would be grey and dull and life-less. What we have to show the world is that we can celebrate, we can enjoy a good party for its own sake, but without succumbing to the temptation to materialism. At the basis of such a Christian perspective is the spirit of gratitude and generosity. Christ has freed us from the power of materialism, therefore we can have a generous attitude to the poor and to ourselves.

Even when we do try honestly to dedicate all we have to God we can sometimes be guilty of self-deception. One of the greatest dangers in this area is the biblical principle of steward-ship because it can so easily be used to cover up our own need for false security. When we sell a house or a car, for instance, we could argue that it is good stewardship to go for the best price. But the Bible makes it clear that this is a mistaken view because good stewardship includes the idea of being liberal to those who are disadvantaged. Indeed, the Old Testament teaches that it is wrong to go for the last penny or the last grain of wheat in the field. We must also realise for whom stewardship exists. We are tempted to think that it is for the benefit of those who are near and dear to us, and such a view is strengthened by the biblical command for us to provide properly for our families, but in the end stewardship is for God and for the poor. We can only avoid the worship of Behemoth if we build on this foundation.

Lest such an approach should seem patronising to the poor, we need to understand the true nature of Christian compassion. Clearly, 'bottle-top' Christianity will not do. There is nothing wrong with collecting the aluminium tops from our British milk bottles so that they can be recycled and the proceeds given to a good cause, but if this is the extent of our concern for the poor then it is totally inadequate. Even if the extent of our concern is much greater and we give in really sacrificial ways to the underprivileged, our compassion is still not Christian compassion if it keeps the poor at a distance. Genuine Christian compassion is always incarnational compassion. It is sitting alongside the poor and disadvantaged and sharing with them not only our money but our hearts as well. In her work among the poor in Calcutta and elsewhere, Mother Teresa testifies to the truth that we meet Christ himself when we meet the poor, when we embrace this kind of compassion we discover that we are all poor and in need of the sheer grace of God.

When I was asked to take charge of an inner-city parish in Liverpool my wife and I decided not to live in the large Victorian vicarage which was actually just outside the parish. We felt that it would be much more appropriate to live in an ordinary two-up two-down terraced house near the church. At first our little house, like many others in the area, had no bathroom and only an outside toilet. Like others too, we had to go through the process of applying for an improvement grant and moving out again while the renovations were being done. Even after the work was complete the roof still leaked and the holes in the 'new' bathroom wall gave us a good view of the River Mersey. Living as our parishioners lived, going through the same disruptive process of so-called renovation, experiencing the same frustration and disappointment, all this helped us to get under the skin of the parish and its people. Some people said we were slumming it just for effect, but on our part it grew out of a desire for true compassion and fellowship with the people we were trying to evangelise and pastor.

The call to incarnational compassion is a hard one and most of us fight shy of it. Living in our materialistic culture we are trained to be suspicious of anything that suggests letting go of things, so true compassion seems a very heavy and unpleasant demand. Our culture blinds us to the fact that only by letting go can we find our true salvation, and so we prefer the kind of Christianity which protects us from the real world and shelters us from our losses. The temptation which faces Western

Christianity is to turn our faith into a kind of hallucinogen which alleviates the pain of living in a broken world. Like all drugs, however, we need higher and higher doses and the result of high dosage with this particular drug is that we come to believe, through Behemoth, that Leviathan is God.

In Revelation 13:17 John reminds us that it is in the market-place that the mark of the Beast is ultimately required for it is there that our true allegiances are tested. Paul also discovered this on his missionary journeys. In Ephesus there was a silversmith named Demetrius who made a living out of selling silver shrines of the goddess Artemis. As soon as he realised that Paul's gospel of a God not made with hands would ruin him, he instigated a riot to protect his financial interests. His chant was 'great is Artemis of the Ephesians!' But such loyalty to his traditional god only thinly veiled his self-interest. In Philippi Paul released a slave girl from bondage to an evil spirit who enabled her to tell fortunes. But when her owners saw that their hope of gain had gone, they sent for the magistrates who beat Paul and Silas and threw them into prison. Their self-interest was exposed when Paul demonstrated that the spiritual and emotional health of this slave was more important than the values of the market-place.

Rather than face the complexity of living in the market-place, some Christians believe they can opt out by hiding behind the doctrine of predestination. They claim immunity to the worship of the Beast by appealing to the experience of being born again. At first sight John's words in Revelation 13:8 about those whose names are written in the Lamb's Book of Life seem to confirm this assurance of immunity, but a more careful reading will show that this is not the case. John's concern here is to show the seductiveness of Beast worship. The Book of Life is a symbolic way of saying that it is only by the grace of God that we can be saved from bowing down to the Beast. All human beings will worship the Beast, and only those who rely on God's grace will be kept from it. From this it is clear that John is not saying that those who are born again are immune. Rather, he is saying that we should all fear in case we fall prey to this temptation, and that this fear should point us to our only hope, God himself. Such an interpretation fits in with the promise to the conquerors which is repeated in each of the letters to the seven churches. These conquerors do not earn their right to sit with Christ on his throne by their own merit and effort, but by their reliance upon God who is the inspiration of their deeds of courage.

This interpretation of John's prophetic vision warns us not to condemn others. No matter how dedicated I am to the cause of the poor, and no matter how free I feel myself to be from the worship of materialism, I cannot point the finger of judgement at another. I must realise that it is not my own integrity that saves me, but the grace of God alone.

Refusal to worship materialism is not the same as having a negative view of our Western culture. The Christian gospel calls all cultures into question, but this does not mean that all cultures are intrinsically evil. Human cultures in all their variety are part of the created order and they are therefore to be enjoyed and celebrated with thankfulness. The only warning that John gives is that they are never to be worshipped, for this is to debase them to the bestial.

The Millennium

One story ends
Revelation chapters 19–20

CHAPTER TWELVE

MY KIND OF WAR

THE GREAT ENGLISH COMEDIAN Tony Hancock is having an exciting evening at home reading a Johnny Oxford detective story. He is on tenterhooks waiting to discover who-dun-it, but he resists the temptation to turn to the last page and cheat. Instead he prefers to let the tension mount as the story unfolds. By the time he comes to the penultimate page he is at fever pitch, but when he turns over he discovers that the final page has been torn out.

By now it's the middle of the night, but he can't sleep. After a while the bright idea dawns that he can play detective himself. He has all the salient facts in the book, therefore he should be able to deduce who the culprit is. He starts to work through the book again and comes up with the idea that it might be Jocelyn Knockersbury, but then he remembers that she was bumped off in chapter 3 by someone who poured water over her electric typewriter. Puzzle as he might he cannot find the murderer, but by now he's hooked, he must find the solution.

The next day he discovers the name of the previous borrower from the librarian. He sets out to find this Mr Proctor of Oil Drum Lane only to discover that he has been haunted by the same mystery for the last nine years because the book was similarly mutilated when he borrowed it. His next ploy is to find the author of the book, Mr D'Arcy Sarto, but just as he is about to press the doorbell he notices a plaque on the wall recording the author's death in 1949. In final desperation he finds another copy of the book in the British Library. He turns to the last page, which is most definitely intact, only to discover a publisher's note to the effect that the author died before he could complete the novel.

The Book of Revelation is rather like a detective story. It builds up with mounting tension and vivid imagery towards the last great event of history, the Battle of Armageddon. As we read we begin to anticipate the scene of this final show-down. We imagine the great battle cries of the two opposing armies, the bloody clash of weapons, the heroic actions of the saints, and the grinding of the last enemy into the dust. But eagerly turning to chapter 19 our expectations are dashed because we find something like the publisher's note at the end of Hancock's book. To feel the force of this we need to review the plot as it moves towards its climax.

In chapter 13 Leviathan rises from the sea and Behemoth rises from the land. Chapter 14 sees the marking of the 144,000 martyrs who have not defiled themselves with women (an Old Testament image meaning that they are dedicated for battle). Then come two reapings of the earth by angels with sickles in their hands. Chapters 15 and 16 describe the seven last plagues which come upon those who have the mark of the Beast. Tension mounts as the world is overshadowed by Armageddon.

John uses the symbolism of the plagues of Egypt, but his pictures are so terrifyingly modern that they speak of all that we are afraid of today. The sea dies because of the build-up of pollution. The sun scorches because of the breakdown of the ozone layer and thus produces skin cancer. There are pictures, too, of nuclear holocaust and nuclear winter. Chapter 18 goes on to describe the fall of Babylon in terms which could be interpreted as implying world economic collapse. Verse 19 announces that all this will happen within the space of a single hour. We know that in a single nuclear exchange the earth could be devastated within sixty minutes. We also know that with the speed of modern communications and the interlinking of financial systems total economic collapse could come equally suddenly. Revelation begins to seem like a horror movie written especially for our times.

In chapter 19 verse 11 the army of God is mustered and the Messiah and the martyrs brandish their swords. In verse 19 the army of the Beast is mustered and the scene is now set for the final battle. Because of all that has led up to this moment we anticipate a spectacular finale to the drama, but all we read is this: 'And the beast was captured, and with it the false prophet. . . . These two were thrown alive into the lake of fire that burns with sulphur. And the rest were slain by the sword of him who sits upon the horse, the sword that issues from his mouth; and all the birds were gorged with their flesh' (Rev 19:20–21).

This is a singularly undramatic ending to human history. Even before the battle proper starts, the generals are captured and banished, and the army, now left leaderless, is soon mopped up. How can we explain this apparent anticlimax? The lack of blood and gore and the silence of steel against steel enshrines a most glorious truth: God's victory is not a victory made in the image of man. The war of Armageddon is another instance of John taking a familiar image — that of war — and turning it on its head. Many of us miss his point because we interpret the Bible in our own image rather than letting it transform us. We must therefore spend some time looking at the way in which Armageddon has been interpreted.

Many scholars in the past have suggested that the clue comes from John's use of Zoroastrian ideas and images which originated in Persia. We can only test this theory by taking a closer look at these ideas. Although Zoroaster's original teachings were more sophisticated, popular Persian religion was dualist. This means that there were two gods or principles warring against each other: Ohrmazd (Ahura Mazda) who represented all that was good and true, and Ahriman who represented all that was bad and untrue. Man and human history stood in the middle of the conflict and was challenged to choose between them. However, the choice each individual had to make was not simple because lesser gods or 'daivas' had chosen the evil way and would tempt men astray. But once the choice had been made it was irrevocable. It meant that the universe consisted of two power blocs; Ohrmazd on one side with those who chose him, and Ahriman and the demons on the other side with those who threw in their lot with them. All the evil, conflict and suffering in human life was explained in this way.

There were thought to be two ways out of this conflict. The first way concerned the individual who, at death, came to the Chinvat bridge. Only those who had made the good choice were allowed to cross it; the others were consigned to hell. For those who were allowed to cross, the celestial journey via the stars, the moon and the sun eventually led to heaven, or the Infinite Light. The second way out of the conflict was that history itself would take a final turn. In the end, it was believed, Ahura Mazda would destroy Ahriman and the world would be made paradisically new. (Later Zoroastrianism even taught that there would be a resurrection of the sons of light to this paradise.)

Is Revelation simply a Christianised version of this much older myth? It is certainly true that John, like other apocalyptic writers, drew on some of the Persian images, but this should not limit us in how we interpret his book. John uses these dualist images, but he turns them on their heads.

As Christians we do not believe that human history and its ending are characterised by two opposing forces of good and evil locked in some gargantuan struggle. We believe in a sovereign God who is working out the fulfilment of his kingship within history. It is because God is sovereign that he does not need to stoop to trench warfare and a peacock display of his power in the way that the nations do. This truth about God is also a truth about power and conflict in any setting, for it is only those whose power is called into question that need to fight. In personal terms it is those who feel inwardly weak who have to force their will and opinion on others, and in political terms it is those nations whose ideals or securities are called into question who need to go to war. It is out of the weakness of men that war arises, not their strength. The sovereign God has no need to defend himself. He can therefore choose weakness, vulnerability and even a crucified death so that mankind and creation may be redeemed. Only the Lamb who was slain has the right to open the scroll of history.

If we accept this Christian view of history then all pain, conflict and suffering have within them the seeds of hope. Not the unreal hope of 'every cloud has a silver lining', but the costly hope of the cross, born out of the decision of an Almighty God who alone can choose compassion instead of conflict. Thus the vision of history proposed by John is radically different to dualism. God does not enter the field as a combatant, but at one and the same time as sovereign and servant. This is why John's Armageddon is swift and undramatic.

Incidentally, perhaps the reason why we expect Armageddon to be more spectacular reveals something about ourselves and our culture. We have already seen that DH Lawrence regarded World War I as the calamity which brought his fellow men's violence and desire to dominate to the surface. But that same desire to dominate, that same drive for violence, still infects us. If we need proof of this we only have to look at the images of violence on our TV screens. The old Western movies were violent enough, but today's programmes make the cowboys' guns look like pea-shooters. Two messages seem to come across. First, it's acceptable to be violent if you are on the side of right. Second, the more spectacular the violence the better. It is repeatedly proposed that excessive violence should be banned from the screen, and such a move may alleviate public violence a little. But the violence we see portrayed is in fact a reflection of the violence in our own cultures and even our own hearts. We must take care, therefore, not to be hyprocritical in our condemnation of violence.

In contrast to the Christian way of understanding power, human beings adopt two strategies which are essentially dualist. The first is domination and the second subservience. Domination means finding ways, sometimes very subtle ways, to impose one's will and agenda upon another. Husbands and wives do this, and so do nations when they seek to undermine the governments of other nations. We often try to justify our action by resorting to weak and worn excuses such as 'someone must be the head of the house' or 'we can't have communism in our own backyard'. But such deceptions do not work. Subservience, on the other hand, exercises power by the act of giving in. At the theological college where I work a growing number of Christian couples purport to espouse what they believe to be the traditional Christian roles of the husband as the head and the wife as submissive. While some of these couples are working out something that is truly Christian in their relationships, others most certainly are not. The wives are retreating into a subservience which shelters them from responsibility and the call to grow.

These two strategies of dominance and subservience may be Zoroastrian, but they are certainly not Christian. The gospel message enshrined in the Book of Revelation proposes a completely different alternative: the strong weakness of God himself.

Another modern form of Zoroastrianism sometimes surfaces among charismatic Christians. In the 1960s a powerful movement in theology attempted to purge Christianity of all 'pre-scientific' elements. The New Testament miracles and references to evil spirits and the Devil were considered primitive and explained away. Instead of accounting for the bizarre behaviour recorded in the Bible by appealing to demon possession, new explanations using modern medicine and psychology were sought. Some theologians went as far as saying that everything in the Gospel record could be accounted for in this way and that, given a few more years of research, science would come up with straightforward cures. Partly because these cures never materialised and partly as a reaction to the claim that science could explain away the Bible, the charismatic movement rediscovered the truth that demons and spirits are a way of accounting for the human plight.

However, some of those who have revived these traditional religious categories have revived a Zoroastrian dualism without noticing it. They tend to talk of human life as if it is a battle with evil spirits. Although they never actually say as much, the impression given is that if one has enough faith then demons may be avoided. If someone does become possessed or influenced, then an exorcist may be able to help provided he has enough power. It is not so much a case of reds under the beds as demons round every corner. Such views owe more to Zoroaster than they do to the teaching of the New Testament.

The Bible certainly does talk of the power of evil and the possibility of possession, but it also proclaims the more fundamental truth that by his death on the cross our Lord has demonstrated his power over all evil. We cannot talk of life as a constant struggle between good and bad, between angels and demons, the outcome of which is uncertain, because that is to deny the power of God. The Bible does use the imagery of battle, and it even makes it clear that we fight not just against flesh and blood but against principalities and powers. But it also makes it clear that there is no eternal dualistic struggle between darkness and light because Christ has already won the victory in his own unique way. The mistake so often made is that in reintroducing traditional religious realities we reintroduce the heresies of the ancient world.

The Battle of Armageddon is a short one because it is primarily fought not against men but against the Beast and the false prophet who are decisively exiled. Unlike men when they go to war, God does not make the innocent suffer but deposes the tyrant. Thus Armageddon turns history upside down because in any earthly coup d'etat it is usually the citizens who suffer while the dictators escape to another country where they have laid up fortunes for themselves.

After his capture, the army of the Beast is at the total mercy of the sword of the Messiah. To understand the symbolism of this sword we must dig below the surface. When John is talking of an ordinary sword, the kind that brings injury and death, he uses the word *machaira*. But in Revelation 19:21 he uses the rare word *rhomphaia* to refer to the sword which comes out of the mouth of the Messiah, a bizarre image which he uses five times. The meaning of this image is that the only weapon that the Messiah uses is the word of his mouth. John uses the Old Testament idea that God's word can make or break things, but gives it a radical interpretation. The word that comes from the mouth of the Messiah is actually the gospel itself. As Paul wrote, the sword of the Spirit is the word of God. To be slain by that sword is to be brought into submission to the gospel. Revelation 19:21 clearly fulfils the prophecy of our Lord that 'the gospel must first be preached to all nations'. Once again John has taken a human image, the death-bringing sword, and given it a fresh interpretation as the life-giving word of grace.

It is important to note that those who were slain, unlike the Beast and the false prophet, are not consigned to hell. John draws on yet another strange image to explain their fate — they are left for the birds. These are no ordinary birds, but the vultures and eagles, creatures of mid-heaven. John takes the imagery of Ezekiel 39 but reinterprets it in the light of the gospel. Ezekiel refers to birds of every sort, but John only to the birds of mid-heaven. For us the vulture seems a repellent bird because it waits for death and feeds on rotting corpses, but for John and his contemporaries the vulture was a noble bird who cleared and cleaned creation. The vultures and eagles thus symbolise the cleansing of creation after the gospel has been preached. Because the Beast and false prophet are no longer able to deceive the nations, the converting power of the word is given free reign until nothing human is left outside the kingdom of God. The final judgement of God at the end of time is yet to come (Rev 20:11), but there is a promise here that the gospel will prevail in human history in preparation for the unfolding of the next stage of God's plan.

Armageddon is my kind of war because it is a glorious war of grace where the only blood shed is the blood of the martyrs, the only sword used is the sword of the gospel, and the only creatures consigned to hell are the Beast and the false prophet. It is a celebration of God's sovereignty in history.

CHAPTER THIRTEEN

WE DON'T BELIEVE IN SANTA CLAUS

REVELATION 20 BEGINS with the binding of Satan and the thousand-year rule of Christ. The Beast and the false prophet have already been consigned to hell, and now Satan himself is restrained. Without the temptation to false worship and the accusations of Satan, creation can begin to blossom in a way that it has not been able to do so since the days of Eden.

According to Scripture, Satan began his career in heaven. The Book of Job makes it clear that his role there was as accuser of God's people. When the Messiah died on the cross, Satan's hold on his position was broken and he lost his place in the heavenly council. He is, therefore, no longer able to accuse us before God and this is why Paul can write such a glorious passage as Romans 8:31ff where he reassures us that no one can now condemn us. But Satan, being cast out of heaven by the victory of the cross, renews his work as accuser on earth. As the people of the Messiah, Christians more than others should refuse to have anything to do with Satan's work of accusation. But sadly, we seem to be just as judgemental as other human groups. Not only do we see this in the bitterness between Protestants and Catholics at the time of the Reformation or in Northern Ireland today, but also in our own lives and churches.

My sister always used to holiday in Jersey. Very kindly she

would bring me back a box of good cigars from her summer holidays. I was still smoking these cigars by the beginning of my first term in my present job. A number of new students, particularly the more evangelical, kept me at arms' length because they disapproved of smoking. I felt as if I was being judged and accused, and very sadly trust could not grow between us. This one example highlights the fact that we Christians are too fond of mutual distrust and mental accusation. Smoking, drinking, singing different hymns, using a different version of the Bible — the list is endless. It is not our disagreement on such matters that is sinful, but the judgemental attitude that proves that Satan is at work.

During the time that I worked in Toxteth a local ministers' fraternal was formed. But because there was such suspicion of the Catholic church, our group was only made up of Protestants. One might have thought that excluding Catholics would at least mean that evangelicals could work together in fellowship, but that did not prove easy. Suspicion, jealousy and judgementalism disrupted and destroyed. It was the same, too, in our own churches where we were trying to form a team ministry. Charismatics would not trust non-charismatics and vice versa; nor would traditionalists tolerate new services. Even more disturbing was that while I saw all this going on, I knew that I too was guilty of giving in to the same accusing spirit.

The accusing work of Satan, then, still goes on. In the Christian community it should not do so because we believe that Christ has already set us free from bondage to Satan. But unfortunately we still fall prey to him on earth. The glorious promise that Satan will one day be bound therefore fills us with joy. The accuser and with him all judgementalism will be tied up and, freed from such tyrants, human relationships will flourish in an almost unimaginable way. This is the hope that John sets before us, one that regenerates us here and now by giving us hope for all our present relationships. For the first time since the serpent spoke to Eve we will be able to say again,

'And God saw everything that he had made, and behold, it was very good' (Gen 1:31).

Behind John's idea of an earthly Millennium at the end of this phase of history, lies the whole creation tradition of the Old Testament. All the major prophets — Isaiah, Jeremiah, Ezekiel, Hosea, Joel, Amos, Micah and Zephaniah — foretell a time of restoration. Though each prophet has his own unique way of painting the picture, the outline is the same. Israel and Judah will be returned from exile; the cities, especially Jerusalem on God's holy mountain, will be rebuilt; the nations will be judged and will bring their treasures and their homage to Jerusalem; swords will be beaten into ploughshares and creation will blossom, and there will be a new heaven and a new earth. These prophecies draw on some amazingly beautiful pictures of a restored creation.

> Isaiah 35:1: The wilderness and the dry land shall be glad, the desert shall rejoice and blossom; like the crocus it shall blossom abundantly, and rejoice with joy and singing.
>
> Jeremiah 31:12: They shall be radiant over the goodness of the Lord, over the grain, the wine, and the oil ... their life shall be like a watered garden, and they shall languish no more.
>
> Ezekiel 36:35: And they will say, 'This land that was desolate has become like the garden of Eden; and the waste and desolate and ruined cities are now inhabited and fortified.'
>
> Amos 9:13; 'Behold, the days are coming,' says the Lord, 'when the ploughman shall overtake the reaper and the treader of grapes him who sows the seed; the mountains shall drip sweet wine, and all the hills shall flow with it.'

No doubt some of the language used by the prophets is symbolic and should not be interpreted literally, but the fact that all their pictures of restoration use creation imagery (that is imagery of this present world order) reveals a fundamental truth. They believed that the brokenness of this present order could only be redeemed by a restoration of that same order. It never occurred to the prophets that the wrongs of this world could be put right in a different purely spiritual kind of world. For them this would have turned the Creator into a cheat who relied on sleight of hand to redeem the world. It would have been like a small child who starts to play a game but, as soon as he finds it too difficult, goes off and starts another. No, the prophetic witness is adamant. This world which is at present in an agony of disintegration is the same world which God will make whole. Until we grasp this truth, we cannot begin to understand the full meaning of John's unique idea of a Millennium.

This prophetic way of thinking may seem strange to us because down the ages the church has often seen salvation in other-worldly terms. An up-to-date example of this is the Evangelism Explosion question: 'Will you go to heaven when you die?' Although there is nothing wrong with the intention of this question, which is to challenge people about the basis of their Christian confidence or lack of it, there is something wrong about the form of the question. It implies that salvation comes to us in another world which is beyond the grave and in a different order. The word 'heaven' is used to mean the place of the blessed after death.

However, this is not the primary biblical use of the word. In the Old and New Testaments both heaven and earth are seen as part of the created order. Earth is the world of the ordinary reality of human beings where history is played out; heaven is the realm above the earth where the real power lies and where the real spiritual battle goes on. In this sense heaven is symbolised by the stars and other heavenly bodies because they represent the spiritual forces that are at work behind the scenes of history. At the centre of heaven stands God's throne from where his judgement proceeds over earth and heaven. Both earth and heaven are created, both earth and heaven are fallen, both earth and heaven stand in need of redemption by God.

This is why the biblical promise is not that earth will be done away with and all the righteous will go to heaven but rather that both heaven and earth stand in need of recreation. Writers in both Testaments look forward to a time of a new heaven and a new earth.

In Revelation, John's picture of heaven draws on courtroom symbolism. It is as if heaven is the courtroom where the true legal and spiritual battles are fought out with God acting as a just judge, and earth becomes the place that eagerly awaits the enactments of the court. We could perhaps use the alternative imagery of heaven as the boardroom of a multinational corporation which is going through a difficult time. The problems of the shop floor (the earth) have to wait for consideration and solution at the highest possible level. It is only as the directors thrash the issues around that a way forward emerges. Some directors may have to resign as their options are rejected but, finally, the solution (in biblical terms, salvation), having been worked out, is passed down to the shop floor. Such a picture is faithful to the biblical truth that heaven is the place where salvation originates rather than the place where saved people go.

The word 'heaven' or 'heavens' is used in the New Testament some 400 times, and most of these references fit in with the interpretation that I have given above. The teaching of Jesus about the kingdom of heaven also shows that this interpretation is correct. In the Lord's Prayer the petition is: 'Thy kingdom come, thy will be done on earth as it is in heaven.' This is not a request to turn earth into heaven, but a prayer that the salvation worked out in the heavenly court should penetrate down to earth. Although a few verses do give the impression that heaven is the place of the blessed after death, when we look at them more closely we can see that they too confirm the other view I have described above.

In Matthew 5 Jesus does not talk of entering heaven, but of entering the kingdom of heaven. It is this message that underlies his teaching in chapter 6 that we ought to lay up treasures for ourselves in heaven. At first sight laying up treasure in heaven seems to imply that heaven will be our final resting-place, but this is to misunderstand the text. Rather it means that because we know that our salvation has been worked out in heaven and comes from heaven, we do not need the security that material things can give us. We are therefore free to let go of our possessions without loss of security. We find the same teaching in Colossians where Paul talks about a hope that is laid up for us in heaven.

In Hebrews we are told that the saints aspire not to an earthly city but a heavenly one. Hebrews 12 makes it clear that the heavenly Jerusalem is not something just reserved for the future or after death, but something that we have already come to because Christ has won his heavenly victory for us. We are no longer bound to the city of earth and earthly values, but set our sights on a new city where lordship is given to God. This city represents God's new order which will transform and redeem the earth. The kind of Christianity which is so heavenly minded that it is of no earthly use does not belong to the Bible.

Before leaving the subject of the biblical teaching about heaven, reference should be made to John 14. Although the word 'heaven' is not mentioned there, the traditional interpretation implies that Jesus has gone before us into heaven to prepare a place for us there so that we may occupy it when we die. But there are two shortcomings with this interpretation. First, the word translated 'mansions' or 'abodes' (*monai*) does not simply mean a final resting-place. It would be more accurate to think of it as a staging-post or inn along the way. Secondly, this same word *monai* is used in the next chapter to signify our home in God and God's home in us. This is not to deny the promise of Jesus to the thief on the cross, 'Today you will be with me in Paradise' (Lk 23:43), but to put it in the wider context of God's mansion being both a present and future reality. The meaning is, therefore, that because of Christ's victory on the cross and his access to the Father we have a safe resting-place at every stage of our pilgrimage both now and after death. The promise to believers that they will be with Christ after death (eg Phil 1:23) is certainly sure, but it should in no way be taken to imply that God has relinquished concern for the transformation of this present order.

There were other writers who lived within a hundred years or so of John who refer to something similar to a Millennium. It is mentioned in the books of 2 Enoch and 2 Esdras, and the so-called *Apocalypse of Elijah* describes a shorter reign of forty years. But nothing like the Millennium of John is found anywhere either inside or outside the New Testament. This could lead us to dismiss John's idea as a personal quirk, but it ought to indicate to us just how important John held it to be. We must, therefore, struggle to interpret it correctly.

Over the centuries a great variety of interpretations have been given to this part of Revelation and it has become customary to assign them to one of three catagories: premillennial, amillennial or postmillennial. Rather than describe these different types (a description of which can be found in most commentaries), I want to offer a few examples.

One line of interpretation suggests that we are in the Millennium now because it is John's way of describing the age of the church. It is suggested that the saints mentioned in chapter 20 verse 4 are the present-day Christians — you and me. I find this interpretation completely unsatisfactory and really quite ludicrous. It makes the promise of the prophets almost not worth waiting for. If this is the hope that they looked forward to then they were certainly wearing rose-tinted spectacles. When we look at the church down the ages we see many examples of persecution, bitterness and suspicion. And we know from our own pilgrimages that Satan is most definitely at work in bringing temptation and accusation. By no stretch of my imagination can I turn the age of the church into the Millennium. It would be like the small boy whose father promised him a new train-set for Christmas and who woke up to find an old clockwork engine with a broken spring, rusty wheels and peeling paint.

Another way of describing the Millennium as this present age is to think of the fulfilment of creation as being made up of all momentary glories that are undoubtedly all around us. The majestic mountain, the glorious sun-set, the piano concerto, the newborn child, the magnificent engineering feat of a Concorde. I can remember when we first acquired a tape of the Lloyd Webber Requiem being so transported by the singing of Placido Domingo in the Hosanna that, just for those few moments, it seemed as if all creation had waited for that sound. All such experiences show that God's glory is flowering in creation despite every effort of Satan to frustrate it. One could say that every time a lily flowers or a rose bud opens Satan has been bound. And perhaps the momentariness of this glory is a profound insight into the nature of God and creation. It was precisely for this reason that my vicar at home would never allow electric candles or artificial flowers in church. They never faded away, they never burnt themselves out, and so there seemed something false about their beauty. Jesus said that unless a seed falls to the ground and dies it cannot bear fruit. He was talking about personal values, but perhaps this idea can be extended to give us the true meaning of John's Millennium?

There are also interpretations of the binding of Satan and the coming of the Millennium that are purely spiritual in nature. When a person is converted Satan is bound, and as the new Christian learns to claim his victorious life, so the Millennium comes to him.

Although I react strongly against the idea that the Millennium is John's name for the age of the church, it does seem that there is some truth in the momentary glory theory and the personal salvation theory. We have seen that John's language is not necessarily to be interpreted literally, so there is no reason why we should insist on interpreting the Millennium literally.

However, I can find no grounds for believing that the momentary glory theory and the personal salvation theory exhaust all that John means by the Millennium. Although I do not take John's one thousand years literally, I do believe that he intended us to look forward in historical terms to a final flowering of creation. The prophets will be proved right. The future of this earth is not one of permanent nuclear winter but an explosion of beauty and glory.

This interpretation of the Millennium does not imply a return to the nineteenth-century dream of progress. That century was one of energy, vision and romance, believing that the industrial revolution, the scientific revolution and man's unaided effort could bring about a utopia where all the world's problems would be solved. The Great War dealt a death-blow to that dream. Before World War I it was possible for some at least to believe in a both/and world where you could have your moon and I could also have mine. But the trouble with such faith is that it radically underestimated human selfishness. It also denied the more than human powers that set one at war with one's neighbours. The truth is that the only world that human beings unaided by God can create is an either/or world where the rich and strong live at the expense of the poor and weak. In contrast the Millennium is a neither/nor world because we learn to submit ourselves to the King. When everything is brought under the rule of Christ, then creation will be free to flower.

So far we have shown that John believes in a God of creation whose wish and purpose is not to write off this world order. The Old Testament prophets affirmed this by talking of a new earth and a new heaven. The question therefore remains of why John mentions both a millennium and a new earth.

The answer is that even when God's purposes move on, there is never a hint of him washing his hands of his original grace. John's argument at this point is similar to that of Paul in Romans 10 and 11. The question there is whether God would cast off his chosen people after they had rejected the Messiah.

Paul's answer is an emphatic no! Even in their rejection of the Messiah, Paul sees God at work because it was their rejection of Jesus that spurred on the mission to the Gentiles. He sees that it is still possible for the Jews to be grafted back to God's vine by grace, and he confidently looks forward to a time when, as he puts it, 'all Israel will be saved' (Rom 11:26). He does not give us the historical details of when and how all this will come to be. Instead he calls it a mystery, but there is no mystery about the underlying prophetic principle, namely that God never simply writes off his handiwork as we might write off an old car. God is a restorer who painstakingly transforms the rusting heap into a beautiful vintage model. Even this present world order, then, will know its salvation. God's final model will be the new heaven and the new earth, but even this old earth will be restored to its pristine beauty by him.

For a long time Christians have been divided about their interpretation of the gospel. On the one hand there are those who claim that the good news is about the renewal of political structures and the improvement of conditions on earth. Such people are often labelled 'social gospellers'. On the other hand there are those who feel that the gospel is about personal salvation, personal holiness and the individual's morality. Such people would argue that the central part of the Christian message is that individuals should be born again and brought into the church which is God's people on earth. Between these two groups there has often been suspicion and sometimes a war of words. Each side has accused the other of missing out something essential in the gospel.

John's understanding of the Millennium shows that both these views are inadequate, and that it is possible for Christians to have a coherent understanding of personal holiness *and* political and social action.

The basic error in the social gospel idea from John's point of view is that human action, no matter how enlightened, can never bring the kingdom of God. It is only God's action in the world that can bring the kingdom, and we can only participate in the coming of the kingdom by learning what God is doing in a particular place and time and throwing in our lot with him. Salvation is not man-made but God-made, and it comes from heaven in an act of pure grace. This is why the central aspect of Christian political action is always worship. By worship I don't just mean what we do in our churches on Sundays, but the submitting of everything that we have and own to God. Worship means praying the prayer 'Not my will but thine be done'. When we learn to pray that prayer in the political and social spheres, the miracle is that Christ allows us to share in his ministry of releasing the whole of creation from its bondage.

The basic error of the personal gospellers is that although they see the importance of personal holiness and Christian fellowship, they fail to see the depth of God's commitment to creation. This sometimes leads them to such a negative view of creation that they almost wash their hands of the concerns of the world. We have seen that the prophetic view of creation which John takes in Revelation will have nothing to do with this. The earth is for redemption and renewal and not for the burning. God's plan is that Satan will be bound and that as God's lordship is acknowledged so creation will become all that it was meant to be.

John's understanding of the Millennium gives us a profound way of thinking about creation, politics and social action. God has revealed his intention to us by his grace, and we now have the hope which we need to encourage us in our stand for political and social justice. I have met quite a number of Christians who have lost heart in this fight because deep down they have come to believe that it is a lost cause. But if we take the message of Revelation seriously, we cannot believe this. The search for justice may be a matter of two steps forward and one step back and even, at times, one step forward and two steps back. Wars and calamities may even make the search for justice seem a waste of time. But knowing God's intention keeps us going. It generates a vision within us that nothing can dim.

This message is particularly important in the life of the West in this last quarter of the twentieth century. Through the nineteenth and early twentieth centuries there was a growing vision for a democratic and egalitarian society that would replace the oppressive oligarchies and plutocracies under which people lived. Sometimes that vision was pursued by extreme forms of communism, and at other times more liberal and constitutional forms. But there seemed to be an underlying feeling, even among those who only accepted it grudgingly, that one person one vote, equality of opportunity, and equality before the law were laudable ideals.

In the West such ideals came into their own during the economic reconstruction following World War II. The 1960s was a decade of hope and vision, of calls for social justice for blacks in the USA and Catholics in Northern Ireland. But today things are very different. It is almost as if the word 'democracy' has become a dirty word and the term 'social justice' a bit of a joke. There is a general feeling that the ideals of the post-war period have played themselves out and have been found wanting. High-minded they may have been, but practical they certainly were not.

In some ways such a reaction is fair, but in other ways it is extremely dangerous. It is fair in that some of the particular visions of the post-war period have proved to be flawed. There are many examples, but the British public housing dream of high-rise living represents them all. Local authorities are now having to shoulder the crushing financial burden of the past. Every generation must learn from these past mistakes and from its own visions. There is nothing inherently wrong in the fact that people dream different dreams today.

The dangerous aspect of the loss of the dream for social justice is that often it has not been replaced by a dream at all. People have retreated into their own semi-detached castles and raised the spiritual drawbridge. A home of my own, a small shares portfolio, a good pension, a decent education for *my* children — these are the dreams of the 1980s. It is almost as if people are saying, 'Social justice was a nice dream, while it lasted, but we don't believe in Santa Claus any more. Let me get on and make a life for myself. If some people have to go to the wall, I'm sorry, but it's just inevitable.'

Such views are dangerous because they are really a denial of hope. They are a denial of John's vision that all of creation will be restored and that the poor and defenceless will have a special place in it. We live in an age of profound loss of vision. Only Christians with a firm grip on the revealed intention of God can regenerate vision for the twenty-first century.

CHAPTER FOURTEEN

NO DEFENSIBLE SPACE

INTERPRETING THE BIBLE is never an easy task and when we come to a book such as Revelation it can seem very daunting indeed. If, however, we are aware of the reasons for this difficulty, and if we observe some basic rules, then the task becomes more manageable.

Our main difficulty is that we read the Bible through spectacles tinted with our own cultural values. Looking at the many lives of Jesus that were written in the nineteenth century, we can see quite clearly how they reflect not so much the real Jesus as the Jesus those nineteenth-century writers wanted to find. These lives of Jesus actually tell us more about the values and culture of the nineteenth century than the biblical Jesus himself. Another example might be the understanding of heaven mentioned in the last chapter. We saw there that the way most people today think about heaven is more Zoroastrian than biblical.

In writing this book I have tried to follow three simple principles which, hopefully, have prevented me from falling prey to the most obvious mistakes. First, I have tried to make sure that the main ideas, such as earth and heaven, are biblical rather than modern. Second, I have tried to be faithful to the consistent argument developed by John. Third, I have checked the English translation against the original Greek. This method is not foolproof, and there are much more complex historical and philosophical questions behind the issue of biblical interpretation, but at least such a simple method goes some way towards letting the text speak for itself.

The first of my three principles has led me to argue that the basic background of Revelation is the prophetic tradition of the Old Testament. It is because this tradition views the promises of God within the earthly dimension that I have argued that some kind of future earthly Millennium is the best way to interpret Revelation 20.

The first few verses of Isaiah 2 describe a new age where God's rule will be exalted and the nations will come to his holy mountain to learn his ways, beating their weapons of war into instruments of peace and productivity. God's rule will be established and, far from being liquidated, the nations will come under his just and gentle rule. John expresses this same truth by saying that thrones, the biblical symbol of kingship and rule, will be set up at the inauguration of the Millennium and seated on them will be those to whom judgement has been committed (Rev 20:4).

Some English versions of the Bible, such as the Revised Standard Version and the Good News Bible give the impression that the judges are a different set of beings to the saints — all those who believe and have been sanctified — who reign with Christ. This is because these versions place a full stop between the mention of the judges and their mention of the saints. There is, however, no full stop in the Greek text and it seems better to identify the judges with the saints themselves. This would be compatible with Paul's view expressed in 1 Corinthians that the saints are to judge the world. It is the saints who initially judge the nations and go on to govern with Christ until the end of history.

In this section, as elsewhere in Revelation, John gives special place to those who have been literally martyred for the faith. He describes them as those who have been beheaded because of their faithful witness. There are two possible ways of understanding John's meaning here. It could be that he envisaged two classes of Christians: the martyrs forming the first class and the rest of us the second. It would then be the first-class Christians, the literal martyrs, who would inherit all the promises in Revelation which are to be bestowed on the conquerors. It would also be this group who would judge and rule with Christ during the Millennium.

There is, however, an alternative way of reading these verses which fits in better with the rest of the New Testament. This is to regard the total self-sacrifice of the literal martyrs as representing the wider commitment of all God's people. The martyrs then become John's symbol for the less spectacular witness that we are all called to give in our Christian pilgrimage. This view also fits in better with the way in which John describes those who are to rule with Christ. In Revelation 20:4 he describes them in three ways: they have been beheaded for Christ, they have not worshipped the Beast, and they do not have the mark of the Beast. Because we have already seen that we are all tempted to worship the Beast, sometimes in very subtle ways, we must regard the literal martyrs not as a different class of Christians but as representatives of the witness of us all.

A martyr is a fitting way to describe someone who will reign with Christ. Right at the heart of the definition of martyrdom is the idea of giving up everything to follow Christ. It is this challenge that Jesus issued to the rich young ruler who came to him with the request for salvation. We must not soften Jesus' words there in order to make his message more palatable. The young man was asked to give up his money, his possessions, his family ties and his social position in order to join Jesus and his followers. We often underestimate what he was asked to give up because we have the benefit of hindsight. To this young man Jesus must have appeared simply as a wandering preacher and his disciples as a motley crew of dubious reputation. The risk that Jesus asked this young man to take was enormous. He did not specify that the young man had to be willing to die for him, but his call did demand a death to everything that the young man counted dear.

You and I like to live in a both/and world where we can follow Christ *and* keep our families, friends, investments and social position. But the truth is that this is not possible in a broken either/or world like ours. There is a radical crisis at the heart of the gospel which forces us to choose. The crisis is that Jesus comes to meet us just as he met the rich young man.

When I was eighteen I felt that God was calling me to be ordained in the Church of England. Initially I fought against this call because I was more than happy in my chosen career, but eventually the call became so strong that I could resist it no longer. Announcing my intention to my parents was very difficult. They were strongly opposed to the whole idea and tried every means possible to persuade me against it. In the end I was forced to choose between loyalty to God and loyalty to the family. This was particularly difficult because just about that time my father had to give up work because of ill health. In a real sense this was a little death for me because I was very fond of my family and they meant a great deal to me.

My second little death came when I gave up my career in engineering in order to go to a theological college. For me engineering had been much more than a job; it was a satisfying and exciting way of life. Being brought up in the West Midlands at that time gave one a sense of belonging to the great industrial revolution. The factory where I worked was the very place where James Watt made his steam engines. For me it was almost a shrine, and I certainly felt that I had oil in my veins rather than blood.

My third little death was much more subtle and took place over a long period of time. My call meant that I had to leave technical college to go to a theological college within a university. This was a different world, one in which the agenda was not only to give students the skills for ministry but also introduce them to middle-class and clerical values. This second agenda was, of course, unwritten. Although it was not endorsed by the staff of the college, it was real nevertheless. My third little death, then, was the call to distance myself from my working-class roots. The whole process was one of asset stripping — my family, my career, my roots.

All of us who meet Jesus share in the experience of the rich young ruler in that we are called to die a death. Martyrdom therefore includes many ways of being a faithful witness through death. It is not just reserved for those who die in the flames or on the chopping block. It means being willing to lay aside all that we hold dear for the sake of Christ. A martyr is someone who, stripped of all assets, stands totally naked in the world for God's sake.

This definition of martyrdom or witness is especially relevant to the political and social climate in which we live in the modern West. The ideals of the 1960s have given way to what can only be called the new self-interest. We need to get behind the spirit of the 1980s in order to understand this term, and one way of doing this is to consider the architectural concept of defensible space.

The great dream of the architects and planners of the reconstruction after the great depression and World War II was open space. Cities, they believed, could best be redeveloped by putting people in high-rise flats and creating large areas of communal public space. Play parks, inner-city gardens, green-field sites — these were the order of the day. In one sense they were an attempt to bring the countryside into the city, but the most profound aspect of the dream was the exchange of the private for the public. In Britain in particular, it was part of a much larger dream of public life. The new world was to have a complete and efficient system of public hospitals, schools, transport, social services — the list was endless. And it was endless because it sprang from an inner vision of community which seemed to infuse everything at this time. The basis of this dream was a new egalitarianism, a sharing, a desire to search for social justice. It was a dethronement of the distinctions of social class and private wealth.

But there was an inner weakness in the dream which has led to its downfall in the 1980s. The cities that were created proved very difficult to live in. The open spaces became vandalised. The flats became prisons, especially to those with young families. And instead of giving new freedom, the public communal spaces became a kind of threat, a no man's land. The architects then invented defensible space. Many expensive tower blocks were demolished and folk rehoused in smaller units that could be more easily defended. Open spaces were chopped up and reallocated to families as private gardens. In one sense the architects' invention of defensible space was nothing but the return of the old back garden. But in another sense it was a tacit statement of the felt failure of the public dream.

The 1980s have brought a reactionary retreat into the private in all sorts of ways. Public companies are sold off to private shareholders, public hospitals are being replaced by private insurance schemes, private education once again grows in leaps and bounds as does private home ownership. Different facets of this process are emphasised in different countries throughout the Western world, the common basis is defensible space. Such an understandable retreat is dangerous, not because there is anything inherently immoral in the private as opposed to the public, but because it so easily leads to an 'I'm all right Jack' attitude which waves goodbye to those less fortunate. Nothing illustrates this better than the general election in Britain in 1987. It was above all an election where those who had employment, those who owned their own homes, those who had recently acquired their own stocks and shares voted to re-elect the party which had strengthened their defensible space. The new wealthy chose to leave the poor behind. They did this not out of selfishness but because they had ceased to believe in the old dreams. There can be no clearer example of the proverb that without vision the people perish. In this case the people who will perish are the sick, the old, the disadvantaged, the low paid and those without employment. But, if the book of Proverbs is right, the new wealthy will perish too.

The resurrection of the idea of defensible space has become the new dream but, like all dreams, it must be tested to see if it is from God. Our definition of martyrdom gives us a suitable test. The call of Jesus is precisely to give up all our defensible spaces. In my own case this was a call to give up my family and career in engineering, and to loosen my hold on my roots. For other people the call will have different implications, but it remains the same — let go of your defensible spaces. The reaction of the rich young ruler to this challenge is understandable and, because Jesus knew just how much he was asking, he loved him very much. He knew how hard it is for those who have riches to enter the kingdom. Our riches are all our defensible spaces.

It is crucial that we understand such a call against the background of the Millennium. That there is to be a time when creation will bring forth its glory shows us clearly that God does not call us to give up the good things of life because they are somehow inherently evil. God did not call the rich young ruler to give up his possessions because they were bad, nor did he call me to give up engineering because there is something wrong with engineering. The prophecy of the Millennium actually proves the opposite — God is himself the Creator of material things; he is an engineer. The only reason that we are called to give these things up is so that we can get them in their right perspective. We have to put them under the rule of God. This is the reason why the dream of defensible space is not a Christian dream. The trouble with defensible spaces is that in defending ourselves against others and against the poor, we actually defend ourselves against God and his kingdom. In his vision of the future Isaiah foretold a time when those who build houses will live in them and those who plant vineyards will enjoy the fruit of their labours. But he knew that time would never come unless we are prepared to submit all our wealth to God's kingly rule.

In a similar way even the public ownership dream of the left becomes a defensible space when it is insisted upon as a dogma. In this case it is not a patch of land or a private house or a personal possession that is being defended but a doctrine that stands in danger of becoming an idol. Thus the defensible spaces of left and right block the way to the kingdom of God.

But there is also another important reason why the public dream of the 1950s and 60s was bound to fail. Looking back it seems as if those who created all the public space imagined that people would simply respond to it with gratitude and enjoy sharing it with one another. Because no one person owned it all would own it. But this vision failed to take account of the selfishness, destructiveness and brutality that human beings are capable of. It was too unrealistic and soft-centred to sustain itself. What we need today, therefore, is not a return to that old weak vision but a move to the strong vision of Revelation and its Millennium.

The fact that the Millennium is God's gift and God's promise has two fundamental social implications for us here and now. First, because it is God's promise, it is sure. This gives to mankind the security to leave behind our defensible spaces and work towards a genuine politics of community which acknowledges the needs and aspirations of all. The Millennium means that it is politically possible, with God's help, to work for a society that is not divided by race, colour or any sectional interest. We need to hear such a promise again and again today because we seem to be in danger of giving up hope in such a vision of community. Secondly, because John tells us that the Millennium can only come as a result of God's rule, he gives us the courage to leave behind the old idols (both of left and right) in which we have put our trust. In this sense it is not biblical to try to resurrect 'Victorian values' or the values of early socialism. Learn from them anew we should, but we must also have the courage to move forward into the future into which God is calling us.

The promise of the Millennium also gives us a basis for a Christian understanding of art and creativity. The Genesis story describes God as a Creator who rejoices in the goodness of his handiwork. It also describes human beings as being made in the image of God. We are therefore artists and craftsmen by nature, and it is part of our God-given vocation to use such creative gifts. There have been periods in the church's history when the creativity has almost been frowned upon. The Puritans, in their desire for obedience to God, seemed to think that a black-and-white world was preferable to one of form and colour. But such a view, taken to extremes, is a denial of our God-given artistic nature.

The not-yet-ness of the Millennium places art and creativity in their proper perspective. Until all rule belongs to God and to the martyrs, human creativity cannot be what it was meant to be. Like everything else in creation, art must be subject to the lordship of Christ. This might lead one to think that a perfect work of art is a cathedral or a piece of sacred choral music. After all, cathedrals are built to the glory of God and sacred music is written to help us praise his name. But such a simplistic view is false. The medieval cathedrals were as much a monument to the power and glory of man as they were tributes to God. There is much historical evidence that prince bishops vied with one another, seeing who could build the biggest and the best. In twelfth and thirteenth-century Europe the cathedrals were outward signs of the importance of the cities in which they were built. In the same way that the great pyramids were built by exploiting slave labour, so our medieval treasures often rested on taxes raised from impoverished peasants and labourers who were worked to the bone. The upkeep of these buildings in later centuries also depended on exploitation.

The fact, then, that a work of art is religious, has no bearing whatever on its value in terms of the Millennium. What determines its true value is whether it is genuinely done 'as to the Lord', and whether it avoids the charge of exploitation. It is crucial that exploitation is avoided because we are all creative and we are all artists, as the Genesis story and the Millennium of Revelation both declare. When my art destroys another or limits someone else's freedom to fulfil their artistic vocation, then it is a denial of true creativity. But when the creativity of one human being liberates another to use their gift, then this is truly a taste of the Millennium in the here and now.

Art and beauty are celebrated by Christians because they are part of the goodness of creation and the glory of God himself. But because we live in a fallen world, they will only come to their true fulfilment when they are freed from human pride and exploitation.

Considering that a martyr is someone who gives up all assets, it is absolutely fitting that John should give the martyrs the right to judge and rule when this creation comes to its fulfilment. Like the disciples who gave up everything to follow Jesus, all martyrs are promised that when the Lord sits on his throne he will give a hundredfold to those who have given up houses or family or possessions for his sake. The Millennium implies that we must give up our defensible spaces now so that God's bigger dream may come to fulfilment. There is nothing wrong with our desire for houses, families and land, as our Lord's promise shows, but they can only be inherited in his good time and not ours.

CHAPTER FIFTEEN

MORE NAKED THAN THE DAY
YOU WERE BORN

D URING THE MILLENNIUM Satan is bound and thrown into
the pit so that the nations can be free from his deception.
But at the end of that time he is released and goes to the ends of
the earth to summon up evil forces from beyond the horizon
(Rev 20:7). Here, John uses the nations of Gog and Magog (first
mentioned by Ezekiel) to symbolise not just ordinary human
nations but evil spiritual powers which the unbound Satan uses
to try to destroy the peace and fulfilment of the Millennium.
John's belief is that behind human evil there lies a deep reservoir
of spiritual evil which, even in the Millennium, is merely kept
at bay and not finally overcome. After the one thousand years
are ended Satan summons up those powers into the open and
their full depth and perversity are exposed only to be destroyed
by fire from heaven. As Gog and Magog symbolise those
empires of spiritual evil which attempt to distort and destroy
the goodness of creation, so the fire from heaven symbolises
that it is only by God's grace and merciful intervention that the
universe can finally be rid of such powers. This is why there is
no battle, no second Armageddon. God acts alone in his mercy
to consume them and he also acts alone to fling Satan into the
eternal lake of fire where he joins the Beast and the false
prophet. It is only now that there can be a real possibility of a

new earth and a new heaven, but first must come the judgement.

Once again, John stands firmly within the prophetic tradition of the Old Testament. All the prophets predicted a time when God's glorious kingdom, his new city, will come in all its perfection, but alongside these startling promises are those of judgement. Because justice is part of God's holy nature, judgement cannot be evaded. This does not mean, however, that God puts off his mercy and cloaks himself with revenge, for that would be to descend to the level of a fallen human response. Rather, God judges from his mercy and on his mercy alone. The first sign of this is that before his great white throne earth and heaven flee away.

We have already seen that John uses the term 'earth and heaven' to mean all the visible and invisible forces that control the lives of human beings in this world order. Earth does not mean this actual planet or creation, but the present order in which we live. Nor does heaven mean the place of the faithful, but those unseen forces that shape human destiny. The good news is that the judgement is to be free both of earth and heaven, therefore we will be judged free of those elements in earth and heaven that have distorted and twisted us.

First, we will be naked of earth. We will be judged free of all accidents of birth, all deprivations, and all injustices perpetrated against us. In a number of the psalms the writer cries to God to be free of the enemy who seeks to destroy him. The plea is that God will deliver him and put his enemies to shame. On the Day of Judgement that request will have its final fulfilment and we will be judged free of all that is against us.

In an entrepreneurial age it is easy to dismiss social and environmental pressures as having little bearing on the individual. The belief is that anyone can make it to the top and that all one needs is sufficient get up and go. As a healthy corrective to the kind of social determination which binds people to their fate, such an entrepreneurial reaction is a good one. People need no longer be fooled into thinking, 'I'm depressed therefore I will always be depressed', 'I'm unemployed therefore I must be unemployable', 'I've not had the chance of a good education therefore I must be dim.' But entrepreneurial thinking can go too far in the other direction. Accidents of birth do narrow people's perspectives. Poor educational opportunities do cramp minds. Inhumane treatment does turn people sour within.

The teenager who lives in one of Britain's unemployment black spots is naturally discouraged after applying for a hundred jobs without success. The process of making application after application only to be rejected starts to sap the spirit and brings on a feeling of worthlessness and depression. Add to that a family who do not understand and cannot support the youngster, then we have a recipe for despair. But it is not just the unemployed who have to steel themselves against the destructive forces at work in our society. Many people, both young and old, are forced to take low-paid and unfulfilling jobs. Mindless, monotonous tasks have to be performed day in and day out for a mere pittance. No wonder minds become dulled and talents lie undiscovered. Working in such an environment cramps the soul.

At the opposite end of the spectrum are the high-stress jobs such as the prison service or the police force. Coping with the daily threat of violence, verbal abuse and the feeling that one is sitting on a powder keg all distort the personality. Such pressures often produce hardened men and women who rely on increasingly authoritarian attitudes to keep their heads above water. They may resort to drink to combat the stress or they may unleash their anger and frustration on the family.

A political stance which denies such binding realities is not Christian, because it belittles the value of Christ's death on the cross. The central witness of the New Testament is that Christ died to free us from these bondages, and it is only by claiming his death that the promise of that freedom can be ours. To suggest that all we need to do is help ourselves or take a course in positive thinking is an evil lie.

Second, we will be naked of heaven. In the ancient world heaven meant the unseen forces that shape and control human destiny. As in modern astrology the stars of heaven were thought to control the circumstances of life. People looked for signs and omens as a way of discovering what their fate would be. Each star represented a god who used his or her influence to control human affairs. This is why there was such a close association between astrology, idolatry and polytheism. The name of the Greek god Uranos originally came from the same word for heaven. The writers of the New Testament did not object that such a way of thinking was false. Instead they proclaimed an Almighty God to whom even the stars must bend the knee. Their belief was that human life was not controlled by fate, but was subject to a merciful and com-passionate Father. Such a message was a true liberation for the ancient world. Bondage to the stars was replaced by a living relationship with a personal God. It is against the background of astrology that Paul declares that it is for freedom that Christ has set us free.

The temptation to astrology is still with us today, but the message of an Almighty God above the stars is far more than an antidote to fortune tellers. It means that all forces that bind and cripple us have been made subject to Christ once and for all. John reminds us that such forces are real and that they powerfully distort our human life, but he also announces that Christ has put them firmly in their place. In his portrayal of judgement he tells us that we shall be judged naked of all our bondages.

In talking of these destructive forces within the context of earth and heaven, John is acknowledging that they are more than just psychological traps — they are diabolical traps. In so naming them he gives us a defence against them. For example, there exists a popular view of psychology to the effect that all the problems we now face are the result of bad parenting or even bad grandparenting and that there is nothing that can be done about them except to live with them. By designating such forces as diabolical, John at once brings them within the sphere of Christ's work on the cross. When Christ died he took those powers captive and gave us the hope of freedom from them. Such hope is not the naïve kind which implies that if we simply say a prayer the problems will go away. Rather it is the deep kind of hope which acknowledges the depth of the evil but, at the same time, the even greater victory of the cross.

Our human lives are, then, distorted and bound by seen and unseen forces. Even when we feel free or claim to be free, these forces trap us. Indeed, it is often those who deny such bondage who are the most trapped of all. Our mental captors cripple us and destroy those around us to the extent that we don't know who we are or who we're meant to be. Like feet that have been pinched for years in ill-fitting shoes, we become ugly and disfigured. But at the judgement God will take off those shoes for us and for the first time in our lives we will be free to see what we were meant to be. We will indeed be more naked than the day that we were born because even at birth we are bound by circumstance. The Day of Judgement will be the first day that I have been allowed to be truly me.

However, the danger with such a view of human life is that it could undermine our sense of responsibility and thus lead to further despair. The unemployed teenager might be tempted not to make the one hundred and first application. The low-paid, under-employed worker might just give up the effort to stay alive mentally. And the highly stressed policeman might double the drink intake and turn into an alcoholic. But such fatalism is totally foreign to John and he asserts as much by repeating that all the dead will be judged by their deeds. Human responsibility is therefore an awesome thing.

John begins by telling us that books are opened as the dead stand before the great white throne. It seems best to understand these books as the ledgers in which the good and bad deeds of each person have been recorded. We know that this view was held by the people of John's day, and many Jews believed that these ledgers contained the credits of the times when the Law had been upheld and the debits of the times when it had been infringed. But it is clear that these books are superceded by the Lamb's Book of Life. It is the book that will prove crucial, and several things need to be said about it.

Psalm 69:28 describes the Book of Life as the register of those who have been found righteous. In Isaiah 4:3 a similar register of saints is mentioned within the description of the remnant who have remained faithful to God after going through the time of trial. Daniel 12:1 also refers to this book, and we are told that all whose names are written in it will be preserved during the great tribulation. Malachi 3:16 talks of such a register for those who fear the Lord and continue to honour his name. Outside of the Old Testament, references to this book are also found in Jubilees and 1 Enoch. Jubilees goes further in hinting at not just a Book of Life but also a Book of Destruction.

Throughout these references a clear pattern begins to emerge. The Book of Life is no ordinary book recording day-to-day good deeds. Rather it is the register of those who remained faithful in the time of trial. The Book of Life is a book for a time of crisis, a time of testing. Jesus' encounter with the rich young ruler illustrates this perfectly. The young man had kept the commandments with all integrity and we gather from the Gospel account that he was sincere in all things. But when he came to Jesus asking the question about eternal life he came face to face with his crisis. Jesus told him to give away all he possessed and to come and follow him. The crunch question was no longer about his day-to-day observance of the Law, but of what he made of this man Jesus and his word. This fits in well with the central theme of the Gospel of John where Jesus repeatedly says that his presence brings a crisis of judgement. Jesus does not actually judge, rather those who meet him are judged by their response to him. Those who respond with faith and trust have already passed from judgement to eternal life. This crisis faced the rich young ruler. We do not know the outcome. Certainly he went away sorrowful at first but as Jesus reminds us in the parable of the two sons (Mt 21:28), it is the final response that matters.

In Revelation the Book of Life is also connected to a crisis — the impending persecution of the church. This will be a time of testing and sifting, hence the apparently strange list of those who will be judged unworthy of the kingdom (Rev 21:8). Top of the list are the cowardly. In a time of crisis the crucial virtue is courage. Christians facing the lions needed courage; the rich young ruler needed courage; today we need courage in overcoming the temptation to conform to the secular values of our culture. Sorcery, idolatry and fornication also appear in the list because they represent the sins of those who ally themselves with the Beast and worship it. Murderers are also mentioned because they slay those who will not worship the Beast.

The Lamb's Book of Life is the promise of God's protection and deliverance in a time of trial to all those who have responded to the crisis of Christ's call. This call penetrates the very depths of all those who hear it. Our response lays bare our true motivation and our true values. In the gospel we are told that only those who have heard and learned from the Father come to the Son. In other words, the crisis brought on by the presence of the Son reveals the truth about our innermost being. But having responded to the Son our names are written in the Book of the Living as a sign of God's absolute protection and grace.

All this means that the Book of Life is not a symbol of predestination. In his first reference to this book in Revelation 3:5, John makes it clear that names can be blotted out of it. The same point is made in Hebrews 6:4 where we are told that it is impossible to restore again a person who has once responded to Christ and then committed apostasy. The Book of Life is not some heavenly guarantee of our immunity from danger. Rather it is God's guarantee of his grace and power to those who believe. We may withdraw our allegiance to God, but his allegiance to us is total.

However, the judgement scene in Revelation is profoundly optimistic. We have already seen that we will be judged free of earth and heaven. In addition, John writes of the Book of Life. '*If* any one's name was not found written. . . .' (Rev 20:15, my italics). The force of this word 'if' is very important. It means that John believes that in advance of God's judgement no one can predict who will be saved and if any will go into the lake of fire. We must therefore leave the judgement totally in the hands of God. John is not a universalist who believes that everyone will be saved in the end, but neither is he a particularist believing that only some will be saved. Both alternatives are declared heresies by John's use of this little word 'if'. This is exactly as it should be, for to believe anything else is to bring human values and human opinions into the judgement scene. On that day all human estimations and judgements must flee from the presence of God. The only values to stand will be God's values and his grace. Faith in God means trusting him totally and surrendering ourselves to his mercy alone.

John's description of judgement fits in exactly with Paul's picture of justification. Paul repeatedly claims, against the Pharisees, that we stand or fall before God not on the basis of our good deeds but on the basis of God's grace and favour alone. Some of his contemporaries said that this was tantamount to saying we can do what we like and God will still accept us. Paul's reply was that such people had misunderstood the nature of God's mercy and our responsibility. This is exactly what John conveys in the more symbolic language of his judgement scene.

Only when the judgement is complete and the values of the first heaven and earth have been made subject to God, does the possibility of a completely new start emerge. John promises a new heaven and a new earth, and this is the ultimate hope that lies before us if only we have eyes to see and ears to hear.

BIBLIOGRAPHY

Commentaries on the Book of Revelation

Caird, CB. *A Commentary on the Revelation of St John the Divine*. A & C Black: London, 1966.

Beckwith, I. *The Apocalypse of John*. Baker: Grand Rapids, MI, 1967.

Court, J. *Myth and History in the Book of Revelation*. SPCK: London, 1979.

Guthrie, D. *The Relevance of John's Apocalypse*. Paternoster: Exeter, 1987.

Preston, R and Hanson A. *Revelation*. SCM: London, 1949.

Sweet, J. *Revelation*. SCM: London, 1979.

Wilcock, M. *I Saw Heaven Opened*. InterVarsity Press: Leicester, 1975.

Reference

Kittel, G (ed) and Bromiley, G (tr). *Theological Dictionary of the New Testament*. Eerdmans: Grand Rapids, MI, 1965.

Other Books

Barratt, CK. *The First Epistle to the Corinthians*. A & C Black: London, 1968.

Camus, A (tr Gilbert, S). *The Collected Plays of Albert Camus.* Hamish Hamilton: London, 1965.

Coffield, Bornill and Marshall. *Growing Up at the Margins.* OUP: Oxford, 1986.

Carroll, RP. *When Prophecy Failed.* SCM: London, 1979.

Cranfield, CEB. *The Epistle to the Romans.* T & T Clark: Edinburgh, 1975.

Golding, W. *The Spire.* Faber: London, 1964.

Goodspeed, EJ. *The Apostolic Fathers.* Independent Press, 1950.

Grahame, K. *The Wind in the Willows.* Methuen: London, 1908.

Hobbes, T. *Leviathan.* Fontana: London, 1962.

Hoggart, R. *The Uses of Literacy.* Pelican: London, 1958.

Lawrence, DH. *Apocalypse.* Penguin: London, 1974.

Lawrence, DH. *Etruscan Places.* The Folio Society, 1972.

Lawrence, DH. 'Nottingham and the Mining Countryside' in *Phoenix: the Posthumous Papers of D.H. Lawrence.* Heinemann: London, 1936.

Niven, A. *D.H. Lawrence.* Longman: London, 1980.

Tolstoy, L (tr Edmonds, R). *Resurrection.* Penguin: London, 1966.

Tolstoy, L (tr Maude, A). *What is Art?.* OUP: Oxford, 1930.

Watson, D. *Fear No Evil.* Hodder and Stoughton: London, 1984.